Alateen hope for Children
of alcoholics

Al-Anon Family Group

ALATEEN—
HOPE FOR CHILDREN
OF ALCOHOLICS

God grant me the serenity
To accept the things I cannot change,
Courage to change the things I can,
And wisdom to know the difference.

ALATEEN—
Hope for Children of Alcoholics

Al-Anon Family Group Headquarters, Inc.

NEW YORK • 1981

Alateen—Hope for Children of Alcoholics
© Al-Anon Family Group Headquarters, Inc. 1973

Post Office Box 182
Madison Square Station
New York, N.Y. 10159

First Printing, 1973
Second Printing, 1975
Third Printing, 1977
Fourth Printing, 1978
Fifth Printing, 1980
Sixth Printing, 1981

Library of Congress Catalog Card No. 73-82710
ISBN 0-910034-20-6

Approved by
World Service Conference
Al-Anon Family Groups

PRINTED IN THE UNITED STATES OF AMERICA

CONTENTS

INTRODUCTION

◆

This book tells the story of Alateen, which is a part of the Al-Anon Family Groups, the fellowship of people whose lives are being or have been affected by close contact with a problem drinker. It tells of their fears, their problems, their hopes and their achievements.

Alateens get together at meetings to help each other with the problems they have in common. They share their experiences, learn about alcoholism the family disease and concentrate on their personal growth in order to lessen the harmful effects of alcoholism on their lives.

They do this by studying and applying to themselves the Twelve Steps adopted from Alcoholics Anonymous. They experience the warmth of knowing they are not alone, that someone cares. Their self-confidence is restored and their hope in the future is rekindled. As they learn to face their problems with courage, they find that their lives can be filled with satisfaction, joy and love.

DO YOU NEED ALATEEN?

◆

Do you have a parent, close friend or relative with a drinking problem?

Do you feel you got a rotten break in life?

Do you hate one or both of your parents?

Have you lost respect for your non-alcoholic parent?

Do you try to get even with your parents when you think they have been unfair?

Are you ashamed of your home?

Do you wish your home could be more like the homes of your friends?

Do you lose your temper a lot?

Do you sometimes say and do things you don't want to but can't help yourself?

Do you have trouble concentrating on school work?

Do you resent having to do jobs around the house that you think your parents should be doing?

Are you afraid to let people know what you're really like?

Do you sometimes wish you were dead?

Are you starting to think it would be nice to forget your problems by taking drugs or getting drunk?

Is it hard for you to talk to your parents? Do you talk to them at all?

Do you go to extremes to get people to like you?

Are you afraid of the future?

Do you believe no one could possibly understand how you feel?

Do you feel you make your alcoholic parent drink?

Do you get upset when your parents fight?

Do you stay out of the house as much as possible because you hate it there?

Do you avoid telling your parents the truth?

Do you worry about your parents?

Are you nervous or scared a lot of the time?

Do you resent the alcoholic's drinking?

Do you feel nobody really loves you or cares what happens to you?

Do you feel like a burden to your parents?

Do you sometimes do strange or shocking things to get attention?

Do you cover up your real feelings by pretending you don't care?

Do you take advantage of your parents when you know you can get away with it?

If you have answered "yes" to some of the above questions and are close to someone with a drinking problem, Alateen may help you.

UNDERSTANDING ALCOHOLISM

◆

What Is Alcoholism?

The American Medical Association recognizes alcoholism as a disease which can be arrested but not cured. One of the symptoms is an uncontrollable desire to drink. Alcoholism is a progressive disease. As long as the alcoholic continues to drink, his drive to drink will get worse. If the disease is not arrested, it can end in insanity or death. The only method of arresting alcoholism is total abstinence.

Alcoholism is a lifetime disease. Most authorities agree that even after years of sobriety, the alcoholic can never again control his drinking once he starts.

There are many successful treatments for alcoholism today. Alcoholics Anonymous is the best known and widely regarded as the most effective. Alcoholism is no longer a hopeless condition, provided it is recognized and treated.

Who Is an Alcoholic?

All kinds of people are alcoholics; young and old, rich and poor, well-educated and ignorant, professional people and factory workers, housewives and mothers. Only about three to five percent of alcoholics are "bums" or skid row

3

types. The rest have families and jobs and are functioning fairly well. But their drinking affects some part of their lives. Their family life, their social life, or their job may suffer. It might be all three. An alcoholic is someone whose drinking causes a continuing and growing problem in any department of his life. *

Why Does the Alcoholic Drink?

The alcoholic drinks because he thinks he has to. He uses alcohol as a crutch and an escape. He is in emotional pain and he uses alcohol to kill that pain. Eventually, he depends on alcohol so much that he becomes convinced he can't live without it. This is *obsession*.

When some alcoholics try to do without alcohol, the withdrawal symptoms are so overwhelming that they go back to drinking because drinking seems to be the only way to get rid of the agony. This is *addiction*.

Most alcoholics would like to be social drinkers. They spend a lot of time and effort trying to control their drinking so they will be able to drink like other people. They may try drinking only on weekends or drinking only a certain drink. But they can never be sure of being able to stop drinking when they want to. They end up getting drunk even when they had promised themselves they wouldn't. This is *compulsion*.

What Are the Symptoms of Alcoholism?

• *Loss of control.* The loss of control is usually progressive. At first the alcoholic can control his drinking most of the

---

* For simplicity's sake, the alcoholic will be referred to as a man throughout this book, although it is understood that everything applies to women alcoholics as well.

time. But he sometimes gets drunk when he doesn't want to. Eventually, he loses control more and more. He may drink only on certain days or at certain times because he knows he can't always stop when he wants to. If he continues to drink, he will finally lose control of *when* he drinks too. He will drink when he would rather not drink, even when he knows he needs to be sober.

• *Progression.* The alcoholic may not drink more, but he gets drunk more often. He becomes less dependable. He becomes more and more obsessed with drinking and less and less concerned about his responsibilities.

• *Withdrawal symptoms.* When the alcoholic stops drinking he may suffer from nausea and vomiting, headaches and "the shakes." He usually is very irritable. He may even hallucinate. This is known as DT's (delirium tremens). In the advanced stages, there may be convulsions. Hospitalization is sometimes required for the "drying out" period.

• *Personality change.* The alcoholic seems to have a Jekyll and Hyde personality. When he drinks, he is very different from the way he is when he's not drinking.

• *Blackouts.* These are a form of amnesia. The alcoholic really doesn't remember what has happened. Blackouts can occur even when the alcoholic isn't drunk, lasting a few minutes or entire days. They are frightening to the alcoholic and confusing for the people around him who don't understand why he can't remember what happened.

Why Is Alcoholism Called a Family Disease?

At first, we may think alcoholism is called a *family disease* because it seems to run in families. Most Al-Anon members are spouses of alcoholics. But they are often the children of alcoholics as well. They may have brothers or sisters who have the disease or who are married to alcoholics. Doctors have observed that there is often more than one alcoholic in a family; for this reason they have said that there is a *family tendency* to develop alcoholism, just as there is a *family tendency* to develop diabetes. However, it has not yet been proved that alcoholism is directly inherited.

In Alateen, when we say alcoholism is a *family disease*, we mean that the alcoholism of one member affects the whole family, and all become sick. Why does that happen? It happens because, unlike diabetes, alcoholism not only exists inside the body of the alcoholic, but is a *disease of relationships* as well. Many of the symptoms of alcoholism are in the behavior of the alcoholic. The people who are involved with the alcoholic react to his behavior. They try to control it, make up for it or hide it. They often blame themselves for it and are hurt by it. Eventually they become emotionally disturbed themselves.

• *The family's obsession.* The family often ends up being just as obsessed with the alcoholic's drinking as he is, only they are trying to figure out how to stop it, and he is trying to figure out how to keep it up. As a result of their obsession, they forget everything else. Children are neglected, friends are dropped, outside interests dwindle, responsibilities are forgotten. Much of the non-alcoholic's time is spent trying to figure out ways of changing the alcoholic. But nothing works.

• *The family's anxiety.* When the alcoholic gets into trouble because of his drinking, the family worries. They are so afraid of what will happen that they do anything to get the alcoholic off the hook. They do his work, pay his bills, pick up his messes, patch up his mistakes, tell lies for him. Without realizing it, they make it possible for him to continue drinking. They don't know that removing all the painful results of the drinking only reaffirms the alcoholic's conviction that he can drink as much as he wants and nothing bad will happen.

• *The family's anger.* Frustrated by the alcoholic's behavior and their own inability to control it, and thinking that the alcoholic drinks on purpose because he doesn't love them, the family turns on him in anger. They argue and fight, call each other names, try to get even for all the hurt they have suffered. The home becomes a battleground. The family doesn't realize that the alcoholic drinks because he can't help it and that he hates himself for it. By punishing him for his behavior, they convince him he is unlovable. And this takes away the guilt he feels, because having been punished for his drinking, he feels the slate has been wiped clean. He figures he has made up for his bad behavior, so he can drink again.

• *The family's denial.* The alcoholic denies he has a problem. He denies he needs help. He promises never to drink again. By accepting his promises, the family is denying the problem too. It is the same as saying they think the alcoholic is behaving that way on purpose. They wouldn't accept his promises if they realized he is sick, and can't help himself. They deny the problem when they hide it from others and pretend it doesn't exist. They deny the problem when they make threats and don't follow through. The alcoholic's family often says one thing and does another. They are not aware that the alcoholic is "listening" to what they *do,* and not to what they *say.*

• *The children are caught in the middle.* As the children of alcoholics, we are affected in many ways. We may be hurt directly by the alcoholic's behavior, especially if there is violence. When he is drinking, the alcoholic often makes promises he can't keep or doesn't remember making. We may find this hard to take until we understand the illness. Or there may be money problems. We may be ashamed of our home or afraid we'll be embarrassed in front of our friends. We may even blame ourselves for the alcoholic's drinking.

Our non-alcoholic parents may give us problems too. As a result of their preoccupation with the drinking problem, they may neglect us, be irritable, inconsistent, demanding or confused. They may try to get us to help control the alcoholic by watching him, keeping quiet so as not to disturb him, going to the bar to get him, telling lies to hide the problem from the neighbors. They may even blame us for the drinking.

It is no wonder then, that we end up hating ourselves, our parents, life and everything in it! We may have trouble with school work, be afraid of people, lack self-confidence, fear the future, or suffer from "nervous" disorders. Some of us have even run away from home, or gotten into trouble with the law. But it isn't hopeless. With the help of Alateen, we can learn to lessen the damaging effect of alcoholism on ourselves and become happy, emotionally healthy people.

To Sum Up

A person who has an uncontrollable desire to drink is an alcoholic; he has the disease of alcoholism. The alcoholic uses liquor to escape from reality and responsibility.

Although he feels guilty, he cannot make himself stop

drinking even when he sees it destroying all that makes life worthwhile and bringing suffering to those dearest to him.

He is emotionally dependent on alcohol and truly believes he can't live without it. He is also physically addicted and has withdrawal symptoms when he tries to stop.

He tries to escape from his remorse by more and more drinking until the pain he suffers *as a result of* the drinking is greater than the pain he's trying to get away from *by* drinking. Only then will he be ready to stop; the desire to stop drinking must come from within. No one can force an alcoholic to stop drinking.

Because the alcoholic is sick, he hurts himself and others. Due to our close association with him, we, too, develop problems. The best way to help the compulsive drinker and ourselves, is to build our own strength, correct our own attitudes, be kind to him, and learn how to detach from the problem.

Alateen can show us the way.

SUGGESTED ALATEEN PREAMBLE TO THE TWELVE STEPS

◆

Alateen, part of the Al-Anon Family Groups, is a fellowship of young people whose lives have been affected by alcoholism in a family member or close friend. We help each other by sharing our experience, strength and hope.

We believe alcoholism is a family disease because it affects all the members emotionally and sometimes physically. Although we cannot change or control our parents, we can detach from their problems while continuing to love them.

We do not discuss religion or become involved with any outside organizations. Our sole topic is the solution of our problems. We are always careful to protect each other's anonymity as well as that of the alcoholic.

By applying the Twelve Steps of AA to ourselves, we begin to grow mentally, emotionally and spiritually. We will always be grateful to Alateen for giving us a wonderful, healthy program to live by and enjoy.

THE TWELVE STEPS*

1. We admitted we were powerless over alcohol—that our lives had become unmanageable.
2. Came to believe that a Power greater than ourselves could store us to sanity.
3. Made a decision to turn our will and our lives over to the care of God *as we understood Him*.
4. Made a searching and fearless moral inventory of ourselves.
5. Admitted to God, to ourselves and to another human being the exact nature of our wrongs.
6. Were entirely ready to have God remove all these defects of character.
7. Humbly asked Him to remove our shortcomings.
8. Made a list of all persons we had harmed, and became willing to make amends to them all.
9. Made direct amends to such people wherever possible, except when to do so would injure them or others.
10. Continued to take personal inventory and when we were wrong promptly admitted it.
11. Sought through prayer and meditation to improve our conscious contact with God *as we understood Him*, praying only for knowledge of His will for us and the power to carry that out.
12. Having had a spiritual awakening as the result of

*An indepth look can be found in the book, AL-ANON'S TWELVE STEPS & TWELVE TRADITIONS.

these Steps, we tried to carry this message to others, and to practice these principles in all our affairs.

Step One

We admitted we were powerless over alcohol —that our lives had become unmanageable.

The key word in this Step is "admitted." We admit we are powerless over our parent's drinking and accept the fact that we cannot control another person's life. We are not responsible for the alcoholic's behavior. We did not cause the drinking problem. We cannot expect to cure it, either.

At first we tend to blame the alcoholic for everything that is wrong in our family situation. In Alateen we learn this is not necessarily so. Worrying about family problems, getting involved in trying to control the alcoholic's actions and possibly taking over some of his responsibilities out of necessity, has left our lives a mess. We're upset, nervous, and can't get our own work done. It's even more tragic when we turn to stealing, taking drugs, getting drunk ourselves, running away from home, dropping out of school, early marriage, etc. We want to be dependent on our parents for guidance and love but independent and on our own at the same time. The problems of adolescence and the problems of the alcoholic family gang up on us and we feel that life isn't worth living, or that there's not much we can do about it for ourselves or anyone else.

Alateen shows us the way to get our lives in order. We start by accepting the fact that no one can help the alcoholic until he is ready. We must remember that our parent is sick, suffering from a disease known as alcoholism. We try to treat that parent as we would treat any person who is ill—with love, compassion and understanding.

Step Two

Came to believe that a Power greater than ourselves could restore us to sanity.

The word "sanity" seems to bother a lot of people. They get the idea that if they have to be restored to sanity, they must be insane. But this isn't so. Sanity means wholeness—thinking straight.

When we're always worried and afraid, when we think we have to do everything ourselves and we don't have time to do the things we want to do, when we feel so lonely and sad but don't know exactly why, when we hate ourselves—then we're not giving ourselves a chance to be a total person.

In Alateen, we find out we don't have to handle everything ourselves, we don't have to be afraid anymore. There is a Power greater than ourselves who can help us. A lot of us get scared when we hear about this "Higher Power." So many people think of that power as God. But our concept of God may be very vague—maybe we don't believe in God at all. Many formal religions depict God as a father. We may have a lot of trouble with this idea and our feelings for our father may get all mixed up with our idea of God.

We don't have to get hung up on God, or imagine Him as a Person. If we can't think of the "Higher Power" as God, we can interpret this Step as realizing we don't know everything and other people can help us. The group can be our Higher Power. If we keep an open mind and really listen for new ways to handle our problems, we will find we don't have to be alone.

Step Three

Made a decision to turn our will and our lives over to the care of God as we understood Him.

When we took Step One, we admitted we were powerless over alcohol—that our lives had become unmanageable. In Step Two, we realized we didn't have all the answers and that there was a Power greater than ourselves to help us. Many of us call this Higher Power "God." Some of us feel this is the group. It doesn't matter, as long as we really believe in something outside of ourselves that can help us.

If instead of trusting in our Higher Power we trust only our own intelligence, our own strength and our own wisdom, we will not find the answers.

Many of us have used God as a gift-giver or problem solver. We have prayed only when we wanted something. When we didn't get what we wanted, we felt God had let us down. We didn't realize we were asking God to do our will.

In Step Three, we decide to do His will instead. How do we know what His will is? Many of us believe it will come to us if we keep an open mind. That doesn't mean we can shirk our responsibilities. It does mean doing our best each day, being responsible for our own actions, but leaving the results to God. How things turn out are His business. We must believe it will be for our good even if it doesn't seem that way at first. If we believe God loves us and works only for our good, we will be able to trust in Him and not be afraid. We will see even unpleasant and painful things as opportunities for growth and self-improvement. When we look at it this way, we realize that this Step can make us more independent. We are freed from worry about the results of our actions, as long as we have done our best. This brings us real inner peace.

Sometimes we have used God as a scapegoat. We have blamed Him for everything that happened when we really haven't done everything *we* could in the situation. We must remember to be honest with ourselves. Talking it over with someone we can trust can help us to see if we are deceiving ourselves.

If we can view ourselves as part of an over-all plan, we will be less likely to get conceited. We must remember that the problem in front of us is never as great as the power behind us.

Step Four

Made a searching and fearless moral inventory of ourselves.

It is a real challenge to be honest with ourselves. It's easy to blame our bad schoolwork on the unhappy home situation when it could well be that we are lazy. It's easy to envy the serene home life of some friend instead of trying to bring peace and harmony to our own. It's easy to justify our mistakes by telling ourselves we got a rotten break. But our job, like everybody's, is to do the best we can with what we have, and all the excuses in the world won't help us.

One of the most important things to learn is that a lot of what happens to us is perfectly normal. These are healthy changes every teenager goes through at one time or another. Growing up is hard even without an alcoholic problem in the home!

In taking our inventory we should list our good qualities as well as our faults. Listing our good points will help us to see that we have the tools to work on ourselves and that there is hope we can be better. We should take only our own inventory and not anyone else's.

It's a good idea to wait a while before taking this Step. In the beginning we may be so confused that we see some of our faults as virtues and some of our virtues as faults.

For instance, we may think we are very kind and generous. But maybe we are really only trying to buy other people's affection because we don't believe in ourselves. Then this kind and generous attitude is really a cover-up for a bad self-image and not a virtue at all.

Or maybe we think we're pretty awful because we get angry a lot. We may not yet realize we can't control how we feel, only what we do. Anger is a normal reaction to rejection, frustration or failure. But it isn't necessary to react with a tantrum! Anger can be put to good use to change the things we can. In this case, our character defect wouldn't be that we get angry, but that we don't channel our anger into healthy outlets such as sports, debates, campaigns for social improvements, etc.

When we have been in Alateen for a while and have achieved some peace of mind through the first three Steps, we can go ahead with this one.

Step Five

Admitted to God, to ourselves and to another human being the exact nature of our wrongs.

Once we have made a list of our shortcomings, it will be easier to admit the times we have been wrong. We all do things we wish we hadn't done, things we're ashamed of. Maybe nobody knows about them, or we think they don't. Maybe up until now we haven't been able to admit we were wrong. But we know that if we're going to stop doing the same dumb things over and over again, we have to start by admitting what's wrong.

This is a good time to try to establish some sort of communication with our Higher Power. We try to think of God as a friend—someone who loves us and already knows where we're at.

When it comes to admitting our wrongs "to another human being," we should be careful about picking the person we want to open up to. It should be somebody we can trust and respect: a friend in Alateen, a member of the clergy, a guidance counselor. It's a good idea to choose someone who's not too close to the home situation and who is not too emotionally involved with us. These people can be objective and will keep us from blowing things out of proportion. If we tend to expect too much from ourselves, they'll be able to spot it and point that out to us.

Sometimes parents or friends expect more from us than we are actually able to do. We can get really down trying to live up to goals that are too high. Talking things over with an objective person will help us to be fair to ourselves. They will also be able to tell us if we are selling ourselves short, expecting too little of ourselves.

It is so important to let at least one person know us as we really are. We all have to be at our best some of the time, and we all hide some parts of our real selves.

This is necessary most of the time. But if no one knows us as we really are, we run the risk of making ourselves victims of our own self-hatred. If we can be loved by somebody who sees us as we are, we will then be able to accept ourselves. Others rarely think we're as bad as we think we are.

Telling our faults also helps us to get rid of a lot of guilt, especially if it's something we've never told anybody before.

Step Six

Were entirely ready to have God remove all these defects of character.

How do we know when we're ready to change? Well, we're *NOT* ready to change if we're proud of our defects. For instance, have you ever heard anyone say, "I always say what I think—tough on them if they can't stand honesty!" Could that be a cop-out because the person is really tactless, but doesn't want to change? How about people who say, "Oh, I always leave things to the last minute—I work better under pressure." Could they be lacking in self-discipline but find it's easier to stay that way than to try to be different? If we're still using our defects to get people to make allowances for us, then we're not ready to accept help. For example, we're using our defects as crutches if we like it when people say things about us such as, "She's moody—don't let what she says get to you," or "He's real sensitive about that—better not mention it."

But when we see that our defects are making us unhappy; when we hate ourselves because of a particular fault, or we would like to be different from what we are; when we have a sincere desire to be better, then we're ready to have God help us.

God will remove our defects if we cooperate by working on ourselves.

Step Seven

Humbly asked Him to remove our shortcomings.

It's a lot harder to ask for help than to pretend we don't need it. It's easier to keep doing the same old things than to go through the hassle of working on ourselves. As Alateens, we learn that asking for help with our problems is not a sign of weakness but one of strength and courage.

Some of us get hung up on the word "humbly" because we have a wrong notion of what humility is. We think it's saying "I don't deserve it" when we win an award, or "It's nothing" when we receive a compliment. We may think humility is always doing what we're told without question. Or we may think being humble means we have to put ourselves down all the time and let people walk all over us. If that's what we think humility is, it's no wonder we get hung up on it!

Humility is none of those things. Actually, the simplest definition of humility is truth. Knowing who we are—our good points and bad, our strengths and weaknesses, our abilities and our limitations—that's humility. A humble person can accept a compliment graciously without acting conceited or bragging about it, and can admit it when he's made a mistake. A humble person doesn't put himself down, but he doesn't put other people down either. A humble person is not afraid to stand up for what he believes in, but is aware of other people's feelings and respects their opinions too. When we ask God to remove our shortcomings, we must guard against the two extremes— feeling that we're no good at all and are undeserving of His love, and thinking that we're able to do the job of improving ourselves all alone.

How does God remove our shortcomings? We will come across plenty of opportunities to work on the qualities we're striving to achieve. For instance, if we're lazy, we will have plenty of work to do; if we lose our temper a lot, we'll meet situations that make us mad; if we're too shy, we will often meet new people. How is that going to help us? Well, along with all these opportunities to work on ourselves, God will also give us *insight,* so we can recognize these opportunities for what they are, and *strength* to do the right thing if we want it.

Practicing the Alateen program is a good way to start, especially Steps Eight and Nine.

Step Eight

Made a list of all persons we had harmed, and became willing to make amends to them all.

Nobody can say he has never in his life harmed anyone. We all make mistakes. And sometimes those who are unhappy are most apt to hurt others. Their unhappiness spreads.

Perhaps we have told lies about our friends or classmates because we were jealous or angry. We may have deliberately given our parents or teachers a hard time to get even with them for something. In order to look brave or be accepted by a particular crowd, we may have stolen or destroyed property, or done things which we really didn't believe in.

There are many ways in which we might have hurt others. But we may not realize that in hurting them, we hurt ourselves. When we are selfish, thoughtless, mean or destructive, we do far more harm to ourselves than to those we are trying to hurt. We end up not liking ourselves at all, feeling just lousy, and not believing anybody could love us.

But we also harm ourselves by feeling sorry for ourselves—just think of all the good times that may have slipped by us because we were too busy feeling sad! We harm ourselves by trying to change what can't be changed —such as other people. We end up frustrated and upset when things don't work out the way we want. We harm ourselves by worrying about things we have no control over, instead of concentrating on our own work.

We must put ourselves on the list of persons we have harmed and be willing to make amends by accepting ourselves and by making a sincere effort to improve ourselves through the program.

Step Nine

Made direct amends to such people wherever possible, except when to do so would injure them or others.

Why make amends? Isn't it enough to make a list of people we've hurt, and promise "not to do it again"? Can't we just forget it? Those other people have probably forgotten too by now.

We know that when we hurt others, even if it is only something as indirect as throwing our trash on the ground out of carelessness, we hurt ourselves. Making amends to others is part of making amends to ourselves. When we make up for what we have done wrong, we feel better about ourselves.

If we want to get well and have real peace of mind, we have to try to undo all those things we regret. It is the only way we can forgive ourselves. It isn't easy, but it opens the door to a happier and healthier way of life.

Many times we can make up for a hurt simply by saying "I'm sorry". Those two words work wonders if they are said sincerely. But if people won't accept our efforts, we will at least have the satisfaction of knowing we tried.

Sometimes doing somebody a favor for no special reason makes up for something mean we did to them in the past. We don't necessarily have to bring up the incident and talk it over in order to make amends. Doing chores around the house without being asked, and having an agreeable, cooperative attitude will do much to make up for past orneriness.

There are some people we may not be able to reach in

order to make amends. They may no longer be nearby, or there may be good reasons why we shouldn't try to reach them. Then the only way to prove our sincerity is to continue to live the Alateen way, striving to change our own personality and attitude. If the damage we have caused another cannot be undone, we must learn to leave the problem in God's keeping. We can try to make up for it by doing good to someone nearby instead. For instance, if we were mean to our grandmother, but she's dead now, we can visit somebody else's grandmother, maybe a lonely person in a nursing home. Or, if we stole something that can't be replaced, we can give to the poor until we feel our debt has been paid.

Step Ten

Continued to take personal inventory and when we were wrong promptly admitted it.

Old faults have a way of creeping back from time to time. If we take our inventory often, we will be able to spot our bad habits moving in on us and do something about it right away. When we have done something wrong, admitting it as soon as we can and apologizing if necessary saves everybody a lot of suffering.

But we shouldn't concentrate on only the negative. We must measure our progress, too. Remembering all the things we have done right in the day leaves us with a good feeling. It builds our self-confidence and gives us the strength we need to work on ourselves.

Step Eleven

Sought through prayer and meditation to improve our conscious contact with God as we understood Him, praying only for knowledge of His will for us and the power to carry that out.

We don't have to be deeply religious to pray. We don't even need special words. We can think of God as a friend who loves us and really cares. We can talk to Him about anything that's on our mind—our problems, our joys, our plans, our work. But prayer doesn't have to be talking to God. It can be just thinking, or it can be action. Trying to do something good or trying to do the right thing is a kind of prayer. So is just loving somebody. Being the best person we can be is a form of prayer too.

Meditating is thinking—thinking about who we are, what we're doing about ourselves, what our values are, and why. We can try to think about God's will for us and how we can best cooperate with Him to achieve it. We can do that on the bus, while we're walking to school, or any time we're alone. Just having a quiet time in the park or at the beach when we relax and feel ourselves a part of the universe is a form of meditation. It doesn't have to be a formal thing such as sitting alone in a room thoughtfully reading a spiritual book for half an hour. If we like to meditate that way, however, that's fine.

Thinking about the day's happenings and our lives in general helps us to put things in perspective. By asking only to know God's will and the power to carry it out, we follow through on the decision we made in the Third Step.

We can do God's will by doing our best each day at our particular jobs—student, brother or sister, friend, son or daughter, employee. We all play many roles, and each role has its privileges as well as its responsibilities. Fulfilling those responsibilities without abusing the privileges will give us the peace of mind that comes from knowing we are doing the right thing.

Talking things over with God is a good way to start and end the day, and a good thing to do any time in between, too.

Step Twelve

Having had a spiritual awakening as the result of these Steps, we tried to carry the message to others and to practice these principles in all our affairs.

For most of us, a spiritual awakening does not mean a sudden or flashing experience of some kind. It usually means a gradual change in attitude. Instead of feeling sorry for ourselves, we count our blessings: instead of resenting what we don't have, we try to change the things we can; instead of thinking of life as a burden, we see it as a challenge; instead of being unhappy about yesterday and worried about tomorrow, we make each day a day to remember with joy and satisfaction.

Once we have discovered this new way of life, we practice it every day. We do this at home, at school, at work.

After we see a real improvement in ourselves, we want to share our program with other teens who are as upset as we once were. We welcome newcomers to our group and tell them of our progress. But we are careful not to give advice. That would rob them of the opportunity to grow by making their own decisions, and would place a burden of responsibility on us that we don't need. We exchange telephone numbers with each other so that we can get help in between meetings.

We go out to speak to other groups and to the public when we are invited. But before we reach out to the public, we make sure we are well acquainted with the Traditions because we know how important they are. They are to the group and to Alateen what the Steps are to the members. They keep Alateen on the right track, and out of trouble.

Sharing our program with others is often called "Twelfth Step Work." It is true that we must have a good understanding of the program before we can start giving it away. But it is also true that, by helping others, we help ourselves. We get to know ourselves better and our problems don't seem so big when we share our program with others.

THE TWELVE TRADITIONS OF ALATEEN

◆

Our group experience suggests that the unity of the Alateen Groups depends upon our adherence to these Traditions:

1. Our common welfare should come first; personal progress for the greatest number depends upon unity.

2. For our group purpose there is but one authority—a loving God as He may express Himself in our group conscience. Our leaders are but trusted servants; they do not govern.

3. The only requirement for membership is that there be a problem of alcoholism in a relative or friend. The teenage relatives of alcoholics when gathered together for mutual aid, may call themselves an Alateen Group provided that, as a group, they have no other affiliation.

4. Each group should be autonomous, except in matters affecting other Alateen and Al-Anon Family Groups or AA as a whole.

5. Each Alateen Group has but one purpose: to help other teenagers of alcoholics. We do this by practicing the Twelve Steps of AA *ourselves* and by encouraging and understanding the members of our immediate families.

6. Alateens, being part of Al-Anon Family Groups, ought never to endorse, finance or lend our name to any outside enterprise, lest problems of money, property and prestige

divert us from our primary spiritual aim. Although a separate entity, we should always cooperate with Alcoholics Anonymous.

7. Every group ought to be fully self-supporting, declining outside contributions.

8. Alateen Twelfth-Step work should remain forever non-professional, but our service centers may employ special workers.

9. Our groups, as such, ought never be organized; but we may create service boards or committees directly responsible to those they serve.

10. The Alateen Groups have no opinion on outside issues; hence our name ought never be drawn into public controversy.

11. Our public relations policy is based on attraction rather than promotion; we need always maintain personal anonymity at the level of press, radio, TV and films. We need guard with special care the anonymity of all AA members.

12. Anonymity is the spiritual foundation of all our Traditions, ever reminding us to place principles above personalities.

Tradition One

Our common welfare should come first; personal progress for the greatest number depends upon unity.

If our Alateen group is falling apart or having problems, we won't be able to get anything out of the meetings. That is why we say the good of the group (common welfare) has to come first, even before the good of any one individual in the group. If a decision has to be made between what is good for everybody in the group and what is good for only a few, the group must come first.

For instance, if a teen comes to a meeting and rambles on about a personal problem and takes up so much time that nobody else gets anything out of the meeting, that is not good for the group. Some responsible member should take the person aside and tactfully make him aware of the harm he is causing. Every member must practice self-control so that everyone gets a chance to participate and let his feelings out.

Alateen is not a spectator sport. If we only sit back and watch, we'll just be watching the others grow. The opposite is also true—if we talk all the time and never listen, we won't learn anything. We should all be able to say what we want to say without being interrupted or contradicted. Otherwise, there will be hard feelings, members will feel uncomfortable, and the unity of the group will be destroyed.

Another example of something that would be harmful to the group as a whole is if the members forgot the purpose of Alateen and used the meeting time to compare horror stories or talk about social activities and other unrelated subjects.

Unity means oneness. But that doesn't mean that everybody has to have the same opinion or react the same way to every experience. Brothers and sisters often feel differently about the same situations. We all have the right to say what we think and how we feel.

Unity is important at the group level, but it is also important world-wide. Knowing the Traditions and making sure they are obeyed is each group's way of seeing to it that Alateen will be the same the world over. That way, if we go on a trip, either in our own country or a foreign one, we can be sure that we can attend an Alateen meeting without feeling a bit strange. Another thing that assures the unity of Alateen all over the world is the use of the same literature. Conference-Approved Literature, available from the Al-Anon World Service Office in New York, is written by Alateen for Alateen and explains the program on a teenage level.

Having a good Alateen group is the best way of helping the members. The Traditions are the result of many lessons learned the hard way. If we pay attention to them, we don't have to repeat those same mistakes. We will be keeping our group on the right track.

Tradition Two

For our group purpose there is but one authority—a loving God as He may express Himself in our group conscience. Our leaders are but trusted servants; they do not govern.

When our group needs to solve a serious problem we try to learn all we can about the subject and discuss it in the light of the Traditions. Together, we try to be guided by a Higher Power in reaching a decision which will be good for the group as a whole rather than for any one member or clique. This decision is an expression of the group conscience, and it is usually wiser than any one leader's conclusions about the problem, especially if the leader is making a bid for pet ideas.

In Alateen, we are all equals. Everyone's opinion should be considered. Our group's leaders or founding members are there to serve, not govern. More experienced members can guide the newer members, but once the group is well-established, they should step aside and let others take over the group responsibilities. Changing officers periodically gives everybody a chance to participate and to grow. When selecting group leaders, the member's qualifications for the job, not his personality, should be considered first. The *World Service Handbook* and *Al-Anon and Alateen Groups at Work* spell out group officers' duties.

The group conscience is made known by the GR (Group Representative) who is elected by his group. Since the GR attends District and Assembly meetings where he has the right to vote on important issues concerning Alateen, and to use his own judgment in these matters, our group should select a person we believe will represent us in the best way. That is what the Tradition means by "trusted servants". All the Al-Anon and Alateen GRs in an Area elect one Delegate who gets together with other Delegates and with members of the World Service Office at the World Service Conference, once a year, to discuss Al-Anon and Alateen world-wide.

Tradition Three

The only requirement for membership is that there be a problem of alcoholism in a relative or friend. The teenage relatives of alcoholics when gathered together for mutual aid may call themselves an Alateen Group provided that, as a group, they have no other affiliation.

In order to qualify for membership, our lives must have been affected by close contact with a problem drinker.

Even if the alcoholic dies, lives away from the member, or is not drinking, a person is still eligible for Alateen if his life has been affected by someone with a drinking problem. A teenager may be on drugs, have a criminal record or be an alcoholic himself and still belong to Alateen, as long as he goes because his life has been affected by someone else's drinking problem. Most groups are made up of teenagers, but may include preteens if they wish. Sometimes the older Alateens form separate groups which they call post-Alateen or Young Al-Anon.

Although Alateen groups often meet in church halls and schools, they are not in any way connected with those organizations. The reason Alateen is not connected with outside groups such as political parties, religions, mental health organizations or various businesses is that such an affiliation could distract the group from its purpose—to help the teenage children of alcoholics. Being a part of outside organizations might also discourage some people who need the program from coming into Alateen because they don't believe in the other group or cause. Members, as individuals, may join or organize private clubs such as dramatics, cheerleading or sports, but not as part of the Alateen group.

Agencies involved in the treatment of alcoholism often want to start or sponsor Alateen groups. But they may not do so, since this would result in the affiliation of Alateen with these sponsoring organizations.

Tradition Four

Each group should be autonomous, except in matters affecting other Alateen and Al-Anon Family Groups or AA as a whole.

Members are free to decide on a suitable name for the group, when and how often the group will meet, who the officers will be and how often they will be changed. The group should have at least one Al-Anon Sponsor; an AA member may assist the Al-Anon member in sponsoring. The members can contribute whatever they want to the support of the group; they can choose to support the local Information Service or Intergroup, and they can give their Assembly and World Service any amount they decide on. The group can be as active as it wants to be, having lots of open meetings and doing public information work, or it can hold only closed meetings with discussions and speakers. That is what is meant by "autonomous."

Alateen groups can do what they want, as long as it doesn't hurt the fellowship as a whole. Just as the good of the group must come before the wishes of any one member, so too, the good of the fellowship must come before the wishes of any one group. Groups that break the anonymity of people in Al-Anon or AA, groups that vandalize property or break the law, are forgetting that when they harm the fellowship, they harm themselves. Giving the fellowship a black eye, or giving it a reputation that will be hard to live down will probably keep away people who need the program. In the end, we all suffer.

Another example of something that could harm the fellowship as a whole would be if a group decided to write its own literature. They may not realize it, but it could have a wrong slant and ignore certain principles of the program. Then, if other groups got hold of it, the distorted message could spread. If people outside the fellowship read it, they might form a wrong opinion of us. That is why World Service is so careful about the Alateen literature. It must be written by Alateen members and be read by members of World Service to make sure its approach is correct and that it is well-written. Then it must be approved by the World Service Conference to make it official. (To find out more about the Conference and how it works, read *Al-Anon and Alateen Groups at Work* and *The World Service Handbook for Al-Anon and Alateen Groups.*)

In a locality where there is no local Al-Anon Information Service to coordinate the activities of the Alateen groups, a group may decide to take on a project that goes beyond its own locality. If so, the group should consult with the other nearby groups so that they can cooperate with each other. Where there is an Information Service or Intergroup, the Alateen groups should make use of it and cooperate with it rather than try to do everything themselves.

No one can ever force an Alateen group to obey the Traditions. There is no policing agency ready to punish those groups who may give Alateen a bad name by breaking the Traditions. Alateen and Al-Anon must depend on the love each member feels for the fellowship, and the gratitude each member has for the program. We believe that no one would ever deliberately do anything to harm the Al-Anon, Alateen or AA fellowships. That is what is sometimes referred to as "obedience to the unenforceable."

We know that if we want to keep on growing, it's a good

idea to take frequent inventories. That way, we can keep track of our progress and spot it right away when old faults start to creep back into our personalities. Taking inventories once in a while is a good idea for groups, too. We can check ourselves on the Traditions to see if our group is on the right track, and correct group problems before they do too much damage. Group Inventory sheets are available from WSO to help us do this.

Tradition Five

Each Alateen Group has but one purpose: to help other teenagers of alcoholics. We do this by practicing the Twelve Steps of AA ourselves and by encouraging and understanding the members of our immediate families.

We can best help others when we have learned to achieve serenity ourselves. We do this by practicing the Steps and Slogans and applying the program to every part of our lives. We learn to understand our alcoholic relatives by reading about alcoholism, going to AA meetings and reading the AA book, *Alcoholics Anonymous*.

We try to remember that "charity begins at home" and that we are not practicing our program if we have no compassion for, or understanding of, the other members of our family, including the non-alcoholics, parents or brothers and sisters.

When we have accepted alcoholism as a family disease we realize that everyone in the family deserves our love and understanding. When we have learned to live at peace with ourselves in spite of the problems at home, we are ready to help others. We can help them to realize they are not alone, that we understand what they are going through. We can encourage them to discuss their fears and problems and give them hope that they too can be happy. We can share with them what we have learned. But we don't give advice; we leave that to the professionals. By sharing with others what we have done in similar circumstances, we allow them the freedom to grow by making their own decisions. Those of us who have serious problems in other areas such as drugs or sex shouldn't be ashamed to ask our sponsor or guidance counselor where to seek help.

Alateen is a place where we discuss the reasons why we do the things we do. We're not there to impress each other with stories but to learn how to use the Alateen program in dealing with our problems.

It's fine to be friends with other Alateens outside of the meeting time. But Alateen is not for socializing. It is a working session. Cliques, gossip and pairing off have no place at an Alateen meeting. If a group gets cliquey, the members are apt to forget what they're there for and newcomers will either be ignored or not feel welcome.

If an Alateen or his relative dies or has some other misfortune, the members, as individuals, can do whatever they feel is right. But it should not be a group effort. Otherwise, we would be taking away some of the freedom of the members who might not want to go along with the project. For instance, if a card is sent, individuals can sign it. But it should not be sent in the group's name.

The group's funds are for group purposes. We are not in the business of making loans or helping people out financially. The help we give comes through our example and understanding. Our purpose is to help other children of alcoholics find the way to be happy and healthy so they can make something of their own lives.

Tradition Six

> *Alateens, being part of Al-Anon Family Groups, ought never to endorse, finance or lend our name to any outside enterprise, lest problems of money, property and prestige divert us from our primary spiritual aim. Although a separate entity, we should always cooperate with Alcoholics Anonymous.*

There are many worthwhile community resources available to help people with problems. Some of us do volunteer work for them. We may belong to a church group, or work on a Hot Line. But we do this as individuals, not as Alateen members and not as a group.

An Alateen meeting or an Alateen newsletter is not the place to publicize the activities of outside sources of help. We might feel very strongly about these outside organizations, but Alateen cannot set itself up as a judge or referral service.

As the Alateen name becomes better known, people may want to use it to promote their particular product or service. But Alateen can never lend its name to anyone outside the fellowship, even if it meant that we would make a lot of money, because then we might get more interested in making money than in helping the relatives of alcoholics. And the purpose of our program would go right out the window.

An Alateen member may work on a committee for the election of someone he thinks is very good, but only as an individual. If the group got involved in campaigning, it would look as if Alateen were endorsing the candidate.

A member can sell things to his Alateen friends in his spare time, but not before, during or after the meeting. Otherwise, people who can't or don't want to buy what he is selling will feel they're being put on the spot and will be uncomfortable. And newcomers might get the idea that Alateen is in some way backing that particular product.

We are, of course, very grateful to AA. Our program is taken from theirs and we would not exist if it were not for them. Even though we are separate from AA, we do cooperate with them in every way possible. We speak at their meetings when we are asked and invite them to speak at ours. Al-Anon and Alateen are often invited to participate in AA conventions, and AA is often invited to participate in Al-Anon conventions. AA members may even assist in sponsoring Alateen groups. But Alateen and Al-Anon are one fellowship whose purpose is to help the families of alcoholics to lead better lives by practicing the Steps.

Tradition Seven

Every group ought to be fully self-supporting, declining outside contributions.

While Alateen groups may be forced to accept help from a neighboring Al-Anon group in order to get started, we should support ourselves as soon as possible. Even if we don't pay rent regularly, we should try to give something toward the expenses of the place where we meet.

Refreshments and literature should be supplied by our own money.

The reason for this Tradition is that if we let non-members give us money, we are letting ourselves become obligated to them. They may feel they have a right to tell us how to run our meetings, and even decide they have a right to attend and use our meetings to promote their particular religion, product or point of view. We have to support ourselves and refuse all outside contributions in order to be independent and protect our right to run our meetings the way we want to. Supporting ourselves also helps us to grow by being responsible for our own needs.

But our responsibility doesn't end with refreshments and literature for our group. All of Al-Anon and Alateen is self-supporting. The money that is collected at the meetings has to be split many ways.

Our local service centers (Information Services or Intergroups) depend on our voluntary contributions. If we don't support them, they won't be able to do their job.

If our Group Representative is going to do a good job for the group, he has to attend meetings called by the District Representative, Assembly Chairman, or the Delegate. His acceptance of the office shouldn't depend on his ability to pay his own way. It's the group's responsibility to see to it that the GR has enough money to get to the meetings he has to attend.

Each state or province that has a Delegate is responsible for sending him or her to New York once a year for a week to attend the World Service Conference. That, too, is an expense the groups share.

And finally, the work of the World Service Office depends on the contributions of Al-Anon and Alateen members. The WSO prints all the literature, maintains an office in New York where paid secretaries handle thousands of letters from groups and people looking for help, and prints and distributes The *FORUM, ALATEEN TALK,* the World Service Directory and *INSIDE AL-ANON.* The WSO also helps new groups get started, and it serves all groups equally. Three times a year, an appeal for contributions is sent to the groups and members are given the opportunity to show their gratitude by giving to their WSO. No contributions from non-members are accepted.

We were all happy to find out there was a place where we could get help for our problems. We support Alateen with our money as well as give freely of our time and effort. This is how we make sure Alateen is there in the future for others who will need it.

Tradition Eight

Alateen Twelfth-Step Work should remain forever nonprofessional, but our service centers may employ special workers.

The help we get in Alateen comes from the sharing of our experiences with each other and practicing the program. We don't hire professionals such as doctors or psychiatrists to come and guide our group. Once in a while, we do invite them to speak at open meetings if they are especially knowledgeable in the field of alcoholism. But in order that they don't mistake our intentions and use the opportunity to promote their own special services, books or whatever, we must make sure they are acquainted with our Traditions before they speak. It is a good idea to ask them to speak on a particular topic, as well.

Professionals who help the families of alcoholics and many others who are interested in teenagers sometimes wish to sponsor an Alateen group. They may be clergymen, teachers, social workers, etc. But Alateen groups *must* be sponsored by Al-Anon members. AA members may assist. Although we do not allow professionals to sponsor our groups, we do encourage those among us who need professional help to seek it for themselves.

We may be asked to be part of various Youth Counseling services because of our special awareness of the effects of alcoholism. We can work for these services, but may not call ourselves Alateen counselors or in any way link the name of Alateen to the service we perform there.

All the work we do in Alateen is voluntary. We do not get paid for helping each other, for speaking at meetings either within Alateen or outside of it, or for holding group office. If we have to travel for our group, our expenses are usually paid.

But Al-Anon could not exist without paid workers such as secretaries, bookkeepers and file clerks. We need people to answer the phone and make referrals. We have to have a central place where the literature is printed, stored and distributed. As teenagers, we can't be expected to put in the kind of time these services require. Many of us don't yet have the training required. So we rely on Al-Anon to do this for us. But we can't expect the staff to work for nothing. If we did, the quality of their work would not be dependable, and if no one wanted to do it, it just wouldn't get done. The message would never spread that way. And the whole fellowship would suffer.

So our World Service Office, and sometimes our Information Services and Intergroups, must pay workers for their professional services. But they are not paid for their activities as Al-Anon members.

In Alateen, we have the common bond of alcoholism in a family member. The example of other members and the continuous support of the group provide us with a kind of help not available anywhere else. We know our program works and that the answers to our problems can be found here. Keeping our group non-professional assures us of having a program which is not diluted with theories and methods of treatment which might conflict with our own.

Tradition Nine

Our groups, as such, ought never be organized; but we may create service boards or committees directly responsible to those they serve.

Alateen doesn't have a president who can make rules, a treasurer who can force us to pay dues, a board of directors who can throw us out for not practicing the program. No one in Alateen can give orders. That is why we say it is not "organized.

But groups need *some* kind of structure, or there would be chaos. No one would get help in that kind of situation. Our groups need officers such as chairman, treasurer and *GR. But these officers are the servants of the group and are responsible for doing things the way the group wants them done, not the way they want to do them. In Alateen, the group conscience is the boss, as explained in Tradition Two.

*Group Representative

Sometimes, instead of involving a whole group in a particular project, groups elect or appoint committees to do special jobs. These could be things such as anniversaries, public information projects or fund-raising affairs. Some groups find it helpful to have a steering committee made up of some of the older members and the sponsor. This committee can help to take care of group problems, suggest meeting topics and keep the group on the right track.

Just as the individual groups wouldn't last long without officers, so too, the Alateen and Al-Anon fellowship needs some kind of structure in order to be able to assist all those who are looking for help. *Al-Anon and Alateen Groups at Work* explains the structure of the fellowship and the relationship of the groups to World Service. Other booklets which explain this in greater detail are *The World Service Handbook* and *The Twelve Concepts of Service*.

Basically, the structure of the fellowship is necessary so that there can be communication between the people at the group level and the people who serve the entire fellowship at the local or world level. Al-Anon has committees that serve the whole fellowship the same way that groups have committees serving them. At the World Service Office, there is an Alateen Committee, a Literature Committee, a Policy Committee, and many other committees with special responsibilities. But they, too, are responsible, not for doing what they want to do, but for doing what the fellowship agrees should be done. At the annual World Service Conference, the Delegates represent the Al-Anon and Alateen groups in their Areas. They meet with the members of the World Service Office and its committees. This is the time when they find out if these committees and service boards are doing what their groups expect of them. It is also the time when the people who work in the office and on the committees find out what the groups want. It is a very important time. The results of these meetings are published annually in the *Conference Summary*. It is sent to every Al-Anon and Alateen group. This Tradition, like all of them, applies not only to the individual group, but to the whole fellowship.

Tradition Ten

The Alateen Groups have no opinion on out side issues; hence our name ought never be drawn into public controversy.

Alateen and Al-Anon members have many different beliefs, backgrounds and religions. If we were to get involved with outside issues, we would offend many of them. And people on the outside would get the wrong impression of us.

For instance, as individuals, we might want to work for stricter laws against drunken driving, or better welfare laws, or improved hospital facilities. But as a group, involvement with controversies and taking sides in issues would not only take away time we should be spending on our program, but could cause disagreements among our members.

Even if someone should be speaking against us at the public level, we have found it is best to be silent and not get involved. Our good reputation speaks for us. If we do get involved in a defense of ourselves, say, in a newspaper, people who need Alateen may stay away because they don't like to get involved in arguments or because they get the impression we're crusaders.

Keeping to our program and not taking part in outside issues helps us to be like quiet, peaceful islands where upset and disturbed teenagers can come to get away from the noise and confusion they may be facing the rest of the time.

Tradition Eleven

Our public relations policy is based on attraction rather than promotion; we need always maintain personal anonymity at the level of press, radio, TV and films. We need guard with special care the anonymity of all AA members.

If we want the word to spread about Alateen, we have to do it ourselves. No one will ever hear about us if we don't let the community know we are there. But, that doesn't mean that we hire a truck with loudspeakers and parade through town announcing that Alateen has arrived! It does mean we can display the Alateen poster in prominent places, such as school bulletin boards, churches, supermarkets, youth centers or any place young people get together. We can put announcements in the local paper about our meeting. But we should be sure to mention that meetings are closed to non-members. We can speak at schools and invite the public to our open meetings. We can call on the professionals in the community. We can leave the leaflet *Are You Living With a Severe Drinking Problem?* in buses, RR stations, public restrooms and classrooms. Only the phone number for an anwering service or Information Service should be filled in on the appropriate space inside the leaflet.

But if a newspaper reporter wants to do a story on Alateen, we must remember to remain anonymous. They can print our story, but not our name. Some meetings have been taped for radio shows, being careful not to reveal anyone's identity. If Alateen members appear on TV, they must be shown in such a way that they cannot be recognized.

It's a good idea to let the local Information Service know when our group is approached by people in the news media so that we will be sure not to break Traditions. Where there is no Information Service, the Delegate can be contacted. Her address is in the *World Directory*. Each group gets one free every year.

We maintain our anonymity at the level of press, radio and TV because no one person is authorized to be a spokesman for Alateen. We must also be careful because we are guarding not only our own anonymity, but that of the alcoholic. It is not up to us to reveal the names of people who are in our fellowship, whether the alcoholic is drinking or not. When we break our anonymity, we break the anonymity of the Al-Anon and AA members as well.

When we speak at schools, PTA meetings or open meetings where the public is invited, we may reveal our name only if we have the alcoholic's permission. But we should explain our policy of anonymity and let the audience know that what we say is our own opinion. We have to be selective when choosing the places where we are going to speak and try to go where our anonymity will not be a problem.

The name Alateen must never appear on a piece of mail that also has a person's name on it. The envelope could fall into the wrong hands and cause the person a lot of trouble.

We should remember when we speak that we may be the only representative of Alateen the audience has ever seen. We should try our best to make a good impression so that those who need Alateen will be attracted to us. We are all responsible for spreading the message.

Tradition Twelve

Anonymity is the spiritual foundation of all our Traditions, ever reminding us to place principles above personalities.

This Tradition means that the program—the Steps, Slogans and Traditions—is more important than the individual members. We come to Alateen to learn how to be happy. We meet here many people who disagree with us about one thing or another. But the program is the same for all of us. We help each other whether or not we agree with each other's views on other issues. We don't let personality conflicts interfere with our program.

Anonymity is not just something we practice toward the public. Even within Alateen, we should sometimes stay anonymous. We can repeat a story if we think it will help another, but leave the name out. None of our literature has names in it or gives credit to the writers. Our officers do not have their names printed on special cards or letterheads. But that doesn't mean we deny our name or telephone number to members of our group, or others asking for help.

In Alateen, we are all equals. This Tradition teaches us humility. It's not who says it, but what is said that counts.

THE SLOGANS

◆

Let Go and Let God

Letting Go and Letting God is a way of achieving peace of mind after we have done everything possible about a particular problem. This is especially helpful to the newcomer who tends to worry a lot about the alcoholic. Once we realize we can't change the alcoholic and that worrying won't help, we feel better if we can believe God is watching over us.

Knowing that God will make sure things work out for the best in the end, can help us to let go. We will begin to see all the things we can't change as God's will for us for the time being. We will understand that if things don't always work out the way we want them to, it may be because God is trying to show us something.

We could easily use this Slogan as an excuse. We could say that since God is taking care of us, we don't have to do anything about our problems. But that would be dishonest. It would be twisting the Slogan to mean something it was never intended to mean.

Let Go and Let God means we do our best and leave the results up to Him. If we have to take a test or do a term paper, and we know we have done our best, then and only then can we place our trust in our Higher Power and allow His will to be done. But if we have a lot of work to do and just sit back and say, "Thy will be done" or, "Let go and let God," the chores will still be there tomorrow. Only after we have done our best, without rationalizing, can we calm down and let go and let God.

Easy Does It

Once we have taken our inventory, we realize there is a lot we want to do to make up for lost time. But we have to remember we're not about to change the world, or even ourselves overnight. We have to tell ourselves to "Hold on!" If we try to do too much too soon, we may get frustrated and just end up saying, "Oh, what's the use?"

As we practice the Alateen program, we regain our self-confidence. After a while, we may think we deserve to have only good things happen to us because we're trying so hard to be better. When things don't go our way, we may get angry and frustrated. Maybe we even lose heart and decide all this hard work isn't worth it. But we know that change takes time. We can look at our problems as challenges and realize that serenity doesn't mean the absence of trouble. Serenity is the ability to adapt to changing life circumstances without getting upset.

We can apply this Slogan to our daily lives, too. If we have ten different homework assignments, we know we can't get them all done at once. So we take one, complete it, and move on to the next.

Although we practice "Easy Does It," that doesn't mean we should be so satisfied with ourselves that we stop working on our self-improvement. Growing up is like climbing an icy hill. If we don't keep going up, we slide back.

At the same time, we should try to be reasonable about the demands we make on ourselves. It is just as bad to ask too much of ourselves as it is to ask too little. It may take us a while to find out just what is the right pace for us, but if we keep trying, we will find it. Remember—the turtle beat the hare!

Live and Let Live

What's right for us won't always be right for someone else. If what they are doing doesn't appear to be proper, it's O.K. to mention it. But if they let us know it's none of our business, we let it go. Nobody likes a know-it-all.

It's not our place to tell our fellow Alateen member how to work the program. It's not our place to tell our parents not to spend their time playing cards. It's not our place to direct anyone in anything.

When it comes to other people's ideas and philosophies, there is neither a right way nor a wrong way. So we just live our lives and let the others live theirs.

Listen and Learn

Many times people come up with different solutions to the same problem. Their suggestions may conflict with ours, but that doesn't necessarily mean they are wrong. Who are we to judge each other? What may be right for another may not always be right for us, but it doesn't hurt to listen. Many of us stumble through life crashing into walls, and this is how we learn. But woudn't it be easier, and a whole lot less painful, if someone could tell us that around the next corner there is a big wall, and if we keep on going we will hit it head on?

Of course, nobody is always right. We all have to make our own mistakes. But we may find that if we keep an open mind, we can avoid making the mistakes others have made.

Together We Can Make It

Alateen is a group. No group can survive if only one member participates. This slogan is a short way of remembering the First Tradition. We must learn to lean on others, and sometimes accept others' leaning on us. We must share our experience, strength and hope with others so that we can all grow. We can't do it alone. No man is an island, no one is a rock. Only by truthfulness and trust can we grow in Alateen. Together, we can make it.

How Important Is It?

Part of growing up is learning to tell the difference between what is really important and what isn't. When we're confused and upset because of the alcoholic problem in our home, our reactions to things may be all out of proportion to their importance. For instance, if we forget our homework, we may get really upset about it, even get sick over it. But once we start to grow in Alateen, we can see that forgetting our homework isn't the end of the world. Tomorrow is another day. In five years, we probably won't remember the incident at all.

We have to learn that people are more important than

things. If we ask somebody to do us a favor and they forget or let us down, how do we react? Do we make a big fuss and try to make them feel really bad about it? Or do we try to realize that they have feelings too, and that maybe there was a reason for their failure?

It helps us to put things into perspective if we think about how important they are. Some things are very important, some things are moderately important, and some things are not important at all. If we find we get very angry and want to pick a fight over something relatively small, such as if someone shoves us when we're standing on line, then it probably would help us to think, "How important is it?" Lots of small irritations can be blown up into major ordeals if we allow it. Or we can just let them pass over us.

Saying "How important is it?" can help us to be cool under stress. That way we can save our energy for the things that really matter.

First Things First

Sometimes we feel as though our problems are just closing in on us. It is impossible to solve all of them at once. We have to tackle the most important thing first. But it's not always easy to tell which is most important. For instance, if we're always doing what we feel like doing instead of what we're supposed to do, we're bound to be making problems for ourselves. Some of us may always be putting the demands of others first and find there's not enough time left for the things we want to do. In deciding which things should come first, it's good to have a list of priorities. Sometimes we have to rearrange our sense of values.

Most important of all is God's will. In the Third Step, we turned "our will and our lives over to the care of God as we understood Him." We may not always know what God's will is, but we do know the difference between right and wrong. If we have to make a decision that involves choosing between doing something that is clearly wrong or not doing it, then we owe it to ourselves to follow our conscience. If we do what we know is wrong, we can't honestly say we're putting "first things first" and practicing our program.

Next comes our own welfare. We must realize that what's good for us doesn't necessarily feel good. It isn't easy to study when we feel like talking on the phone. But if we have a test the next day, studying is good for us. Talking on the phone isn't. It isn't easy to say "no" when a friend asks us to do something for him. But if we know that doing that thing would be bad for us, we owe it to ourselves to refuse.

If we do what we know is right, and we do what is good for us, then we can think about the welfare of others. We can try to help out in our family, in our group, in our church, in our school. Putting "first things first" will help us to choose our activities wisely so that they don't overlap and so that we can do the things we want to do without getting hectic.

In making up a program for the day, we can get a lot accomplished if we do the most important things first. It may be something we don't like to do. But if it has to be done, it's best to do it and get it out of the way. Then it's not hanging over our heads for the rest of the day.

When we take our inventory, we may want to work on all our defects at once. Again, it's important to put first things first. We have to decide which defect is hurting us and others the most, and work on it. Once we get into the habit of putting first things first, we will find our lives more manageable. The sense of accomplishment that we derive from getting things done will help us to feel better about ourselves. Putting "first things first" takes a lot of the hassle out of living and puts a lot of serenity in.

Keep It Simple

"Keep it Simple" can be applied to our lives in general. We can over-complicate our lives by taking on more than we can handle. So we find out that we're late for activities, time that should be spent on homework is being spent on something else, and we end up trying to catch up by cramming or cutting corners or doing two things at once. We get nervous and end up not enjoying anything. When we're at the basketball game, we're thinking about tomorrow's test; when we're in class, we're thinking about the weekend party. "Keep it Simple" means we should do one thing at a time. We have to make sure that our head and our body are in the same place. If we're complicating our lives by too many activities, then maybe we should sit down and try to figure out what we can do about it. It might be better to do less and do it well than to try to do too much and do none of it right.

"Keep it Simple" can also be applied to our attitudes. We can make ourselves miserable trying to figure out other people's motives for doing things. For instance, we can waste a lot of time trying to figure out why the alcoholic drinks. But it's not going to make any difference. What will make a difference is how we react to it. Or, if someone says hello to us when they usually don't, we shouldn't try to analyze why they did it, but just be happy about it and accept their friendliness.

This slogan can also be applied to the way we work the program. If we try to go at every Step at once, we'll end up frustrated and defeated. We can keep it simple by taking one at a time. If we're having a lot of trouble with a particular thing, we can ask someone to help us. If it still gives us trouble, we should drop it and work on something else. When we come back to our problem later on, we may see it in a completely different light.

"Keep it Simple" means that we don't make mountains out of molehills. We don't exaggerate our problems. We try to get at the core of the problem instead of getting bogged down in details. Keeping it simple is a perfect antidote for confusion.

One Day At a Time

When we come into Alateen, most of us are worried about the future. We worry about what we're going to be, about what will happen to the alcoholic, we worry about all kinds of things. Most of them will never happen. And all the worrying in the world won't change a thing.

Then there are those of us who are always thinking about our past mistakes. We feel so bad about them that we keep going over them in our minds, reliving the whole thing, and we end up feeling frustrated and unhappy because we can't change what happened.

Worrying about the future and regretting the past do only one thing—they spoil today. The past is gone. We can learn from past mistakes and try to make up for the things we regret. But then we should forget it. The future hasn't come yet. It may never come. We don't know, any of us, how many days we will live. This day could be the only one we have left. That doesn't mean we shouldn't make plans for our future. It does mean we shouldn't put off until tomorrow what we can do today. If there's an apology to be made, or a project to get started, if we have a chance to do somebody a favor, let's do it today.

Every day is a new beginning. It can be whatever we make of it. We can spend the day cursing our luck, or we can take it as it comes and make the best of it. We can spend it criticizing others or we can work on ourselves. We can enjoy the good things in it, or we can let the unpleasant things spoil it. Even the worst day has some good moments to be enjoyed.

We can think of our lives as books. Each day is a new page. We can make the book interesting or dull, happy or sad. It is up to us.

We can do something for one day that would scare us if we thought we had to keep it up for a lifetime. And that's what life is all about—facing each day's challenges with courage, taking the good with the bad. If we try to make each day a good day, we will be paving the way for a good future and will have a lot of good memories when our todays have become yesterdays.

Here are some things that help to make each day a good one:

A positive attitude—looking for the good in things instead of the bad, believing in ourselves, trusting in our Higher Power.

Time for ourselves—a few minutes to think about ourselves, our program, our progress, our goals, our mistakes, our achievements.

Time for others—time to help out at home, to help somebody carry a package, to do a favor to give a kind word, to smile, to be aware.

A program—some idea of what we want to do that day so that we won't waste our time being bored or try to do so much that we get exhausted.

Self-discipline—deliberate attention to a character defect such as cleaning our room if we're sloppy, or getting started on a project if we tend to put things off, or being agreeable if we tend to be argumentative.

If we live each day to the best of our ability, we will soon find we don't have time to worry about the future or regret the past. We will be too busy enjoying life.

PERSONAL STORIES

◆

The stories on the following pages were all written by Alateen members. Some had a very bad time, others had comparatively mild problems. Perhaps you will find someone here you can identify with. Or maybe you will realize you haven't had it so rough after all. Whatever your problem, you can be sure you are not alone. Reading how someone else has found help in Alateen may give you some insight into your own situation. But practicing the program yourself, and getting to meetings if you can, is the best way to achieve the happiness and serenity the program offers.

I Was The Only One Who Could "Handle" Dad

The first time I heard the word "alcoholic" applied to my father was when I was in the sixth grade. Before that I knew something was wrong, but I didn't know what it was. It was something of a relief to name the trouble, but I misunderstood the meaning of the word. It meant that Dad drank too much and Dad was mean to Mom and Dad did this and Dad did that, and nothing was wrong with the rest of us.

Since alcoholism is a progressive disease, Dad got worse.

I assumed many of my parents' responsibilities toward the kids and became very good at "handling" my father. I knew when to listen to his sermons and when to defy him to get what I wanted.

This went on until the summer after the eighth grade. Mom got very sick one day, and I sent for Dad's sister to take her to the hospital. Dad went through hell that summer, but all I could see was what he was doing to us kids, especially me.

My two younger sisters went to my uncle's farm and my little brother stayed with Dad and me. I was really proud of the way I got the kids and their baggage out of the house without Dad catching us. I was learning how to act like the wife of an alcoholic before Al-Anon. I poured out liquor, tried to empty the shells out of his gun, got his checks out of the mail before he saw them, the whole bit.

After a while, my brother went to the farm too, but I stayed home. I hated my Dad's guts, but I could handle him. I could get away with defying and insulting him and treating him like an enemy to be outwitted rather than my father who was suffering.

After Mom got out of the hospital, she had Dad committed. The kids came back from the farm and everything was fine. Then Dad came home. My resentment hadn't decreased much. I wondered what right he had to tell me what to do when I had practically raised my brother and sisters. In addition, I was very confused. I didn't consider myself an equal to my brother and sisters, but my self-written role as parent no longer existed.

Everything was supposed to be back to normal when Dad got out of the hospital, but no one knew what normal was. I think I must have gotten used to Dad, and eventually I learned to like him and actually admire him a little.

But there was a volcano inside me ready to erupt. Finally, one night, I had a terrible fight with both my parents. A priest helped me realize that I, too, had hit bottom that night, and I admitted I was powerless over my emotions and that my life had become unmanageable. I was emotionally ill.

Now I know my resentments were a major factor in my illness. If only I'd had Alateen then!

When I went away to college, my problems got worse and I ended up in the mental hospital. I had to drop out of school and Dad came to get me. I discovered that parents are a precious commodity even if they aren't perfect. During the next few months, I found out that Dad, because of all he had been through, was a very understanding man.

After a while, things started getting worse, and I discovered Dad was drinking again. Everything I had recently learned flew out the window, and I reverted to the old habits, except this time I was terrified, and the terror made me insanely angry. I wanted to kill Dad. But I left home again instead.

The pressures of school were too much for me and I had to go back to the hospital for a couple of days. I hated everyone including myself. Shortly after my release, I decided I was tired of hating. It seemed to me Alateen could help me get rid of some of my hatred. So I joined.

It was really great to accept the idea that an alcoholic is genuinely sick. I had paid lip service to this idea, but never had applied it to my father. I think that was the best thing at first. A lot of the hate started going away after I realized Dad was sick.

Another good thing was letting go and letting God. I

had given up on Dad, but that isn't the same as letting go or admitting I was powerless over Dad.

Recently I have made an effort to let Alateen influence my whole life. I'm learning to live 24 hours at a time, and it's a lot easier than worrying.

I have a lot of slips. I've gone home more than once with a halo on my head only to come back a wreck. I've dug out the literature and discovered that feeling very much superior to my father goofed me up. Feeling superior is one of my big defects. I find myself pitying my father a lot. You can't pity something you're not superior to.

I'm not certain what I believe about God right now, nor am I certain how I should put into action the things I do believe. As I get older, though, these questions are being answered. My life is becoming more serene, and I am gaining courage to change the things I don't like about it.

My relationship with my father is better now than it ever was. We've got a thing going for us. We've both been in mental hospitals, which is something you can't understand until you've been there. We laugh at the same things, and we like each other. In fact, we love each other.

You Don't Have To Hate

Before Alateen, there were times when I was embarrassed, times when I was afraid. But basically my relationship with my alcoholic mother was good. There was communication and even love.

It baffled me at first, to hear Alateen members talk about feelings I had experienced only slightly. Sometimes I felt out of place. But gradually, I realized two important things. First, I should consider myself lucky not to have been through as many harmful experiences as some of the others in the group. I should keep in mind that *alcoholism* is the common denominator that brings us together. Hate is *not* a requirement for membership in this fellowship. Second, I learned Alateen is an individual program. It offers me the chance to act in a healthier way; to change my attitude from hopelessness and self-pity to joy and contentment.

I've had a lot more trouble getting along with my non-alcoholic father than my alcoholic mother. But Alateen has taught me alcoholism is a *family* disease and that he, too, has been affected, perhaps more deeply than I have. I am starting to develop patience and understanding and life at home is generally happier.

Alateen has changed me inside and out. It feels good to be at peace with myself and have enough confidence to extend the hand of friendship to another as it was extended to me when I first came. When I think of how I hated to be with people before! It's so wonderful to love and be loved!

I have gained a completely individual belief in a Higher Power. God, as I understand Him, is a totally reliable, unfailing Friend I can look to for help in meeting my daily problems. And when I feel my problem is too much for me to handle, I know I can turn it over to my Higher Power and feel comfortable.

I am grateful my mother found AA five years ago and suggested I try Alateen. It is such a good feeling to have found a new way of life with hope, joy, happiness and peace. Being in Alateen *has* made all the difference to me!

Bring The Ol' Body Around—The Mind Will Catch Up Later

My life started getting especially rough when I was in junior high. I was unhappy at school and at home. Even though I studied hard, my teachers never seemed satisfied with my work. I felt ugly and lonely, had no friends, and was painfully self-conscious. Although I cried a lot, it seemed no one cared enough about me to try to help me. Life was hell.

In May of my freshman year of high school, I scratched my wrists with a razor blade. Then someone finally noticed me—I was sent to a psychiatric hospital. That was only the first trip. Since then, I've seen psychiatrists, have taken tranquilizers and anti-depressants, and have had shock treatments. I was so terribly depressed and lacking in self-confidence that I put off college for two years and worked instead.

It was during the summer following high school that I found Alateen. I was eighteen and certainly was an emotional mess. I don't know how the Alateens and sponsor stood me, because all I did was tell them my problems. Each night, after I had spouted off for a while, they would gently change the subject to alcoholism. Although I had trouble identifying with them—my Dad drank at home and did not appear drunk—I eventually got much help and comfort from the Alateen program.

For example, I expected everyone to throw a fit when I claimed to be an atheist, but they weren't the least upset. They told me I didn't necessarily have to believe in the God I'd been turned against by my early experiences with religion. Not until I came to Alateen had I been permitted to believe in the kind of Higher Power I wanted to. By their fine example, and mostly because they were not pushy about it, in a year I was believing in God as I understood Him.

After a while, the program began to help me cope with the problems of everyday living. The Serenity Prayer, "Let Go and Let God" and "Live and Let Live" have been a great help to me time and time again.

Most of all, Alateen has given me hope that maybe I am worth something, maybe I am living here on earth for some reason I can't yet understand, and maybe I can be fairly happy. None of my school friends, teachers, parents, doctors or psychiatrists ever succeeded in giving me this hope. Alateen is the first place I have ever felt truly accepted. Even though I'm still very unhappy much of the time, I now have good spells to give me some relief. I might have killed myself if I hadn't finally found Alateen, and the program has helped me to find the courage to go to college.

I hope the kids in my group are right when they say, "Bring the ol' body around . . . the mind will catch up later," because that means if I keep coming, maybe I can improve my outlook on life even more. To me, Alateen really is "a way of life and a wonderful, healthy program to live by and enjoy."

I Didn't Want To Be Like My Father

I am the son of an alcoholic, an alcoholic myself, and an arrested drug addict. I found out my father was an alcoholic when I was about 12. I started going to Alateen then, but I couldn't identify. I didn't think I had been affected. In fact, I thought my life had been perfectly normal until then.

Soon after that, my parents separated and my older brother was killed in a car accident. Then something in me began to change. I stopped going to church and school didn't mean anything to me. I turned away from God because I figured he didn't do me any favors and I wasn't good enough for Him.

I told myself I didn't want to be like my father, but the more I tried to be different, the more I became just like him.

I started drinking, smoking pot and sniffing glue when I was 13. By the time I was 16, I was doing heavier drugs and was strung out on heroin. Pretty soon I was pushing to keep up my habit. This is when I was busted—my mother turned me in. I'm thankful to her now, because I got a chance to be straight. Jail gave me time to think. But I was so messed up, all I really did was plan how to do it the next time without getting caught.

When I got out of jail, the judge made me go to AA. I always went home and got high right after the meetings but I did enjoy them. One day, the person who was to become my Alateen Sponsor called and invited me to an Alateen meeting. And that was the beginning of my recovery. Now I realize that the reason I didn't get anything out of it before is I didn't put anything into it.

When I came back to Alateen, I didn't want to hear about God or anything spiritual. I still couldn't admit I had been affected by my father's alcoholism. I felt very much alone—so inadequate. I didn't think anyone else could feel as low as I did. But I found a lot of kids with problems just like mine. I didn't have to worry about what I said at meetings. Nobody put me down for what I thought or said. I began finding myself.

Slowly I started to notice a special something that the other Alateen members had. They seemed to have some kind of faith and I wanted it too. They believed in some-thing greater than themselves and I had to have it. At first, it was really hard for me to try to believe in God, but there was no other road for me. I kept seeing these people who had what I wanted and I just couldn't back away. They knew what they were doing, they were honest with them-selves and they were honest with me and everyone else.

But I had doubts. I was afraid to miss out on things my buddies were still doing. I worried about not having any fun. Now I know there are lots of things I can enjoy and still be straight. Believe me, it's much better.

I was always worried about what people thought of me. Now I realize they probably weren't thinking about me at all.

I was just beginning to find God when I attended ESAC (a big Alateen Conference) for the first time. My Sponsor asked me to speak in front of 600 Alateens about "God as I Understand Him." I said no. I couldn't talk in front of anyone. She looked really hurt. I felt I had to do it for her as well as for myself. I had to try or I'd never do it. It was like I had to do something I'd been putting off all my life. I had to do something right without being afraid.

But I was really hassled. I planned what I was going to say, but I kept forgetting. As I stood there facing 600 people, I was completely speechless. For the first time in my life, I prayed like I really wanted help. I said "God help me". What happened was, God just started putting the words right in my mouth!

It felt so strange! I talked from my heart for the first time and words just started pouring out of me. I talked about myself and I wasn't afraid. It was an answer from God.

This summer, my father committed suicide. If I hadn't

taken the First Step in Alateen and had not found faith in God, I'd be shooting dope again right now. I feel I'm off the hook with my father's problem. I don't have to worry about it now. I know I did all I could to help my Dad—I changed.

When it happened, I worried about how it would affect my younger brother because I remembered how I was at his age when my older brother died. But I worried for nothing because he is much stronger than I was, then.

I know my younger brother respects me now and is watching every move I make. I feel as long as I'm straight and he has Alateen, he'll make it fine.

If I tried to tell you all the changes that have taken place in my life since coming into Alateen, I'd never be able to stop. My attitudes are positive, I've gained self-confidence, I feel at ease, I'm planning for a future. But, best of all, I'm happy, and I thank God, Alateen, and AA for this.

I Tried To Kill Myself

I am the daughter of an alcoholic. My father drank the first three years of my life but was sober and active in AA for the next eight years. When he started to drink again after all that time, I just couldn't take it. I hated him and everyone else, too. My schoolwork suffered and I became withdrawn. At first I wouldn't talk to anyone, and eventually, I couldn't. I was always afraid I would say the wrong thing.

After a while, my father, who had always been a quiet, kind man, started to get violent. I would get right in the middle of the fights and ended up with black eyes and a broken nose more than once. I even had to be hospitalized once because I was so badly hurt. I developed a nervous stomach and went to the hospital nine times in one year for nervous conditions.

Finally the doctor told me that I had an ulcer and that I would have to leave the house because I was on the verge of a nervous breakdown. My mother turned against me and I left, feeling like a traitor.

I went away to college for nine months but worked at three jobs at the same time. It was too much for me, so I quit college and one of my jobs.

At this point, I felt I needed something else, so I went into Alateen. But I didn't last long. I didn't give anything and I don't think I wanted it.

I got very lonely and homesick, so I decided to go back home. But nothing had changed there. My mother wanted me to tell her whether or not she should separate from my father. But I thought it wasn't my decision to make.

One night, my mother went out and I was home alone when my father came home drunk. We had a terrible fight with knives and I almost killed him. I was so upset—I thought I was crazy. I took off in the car and decided to kill myself.

I went off a small cliff, but my car stopped just three inches from a tree. I believed it was a miracle and made a decision to return to Alateen. This time I listened and after three or four months, I started to open up.

I will always be grateful for Alateen because without it, I know I woudn't be here today. Alateen taught me to talk all over again, not to be afraid of people. It has taught me to accept myself and my father for what we are, to love him and to understand him.

I Had Everything Except What I Really Wanted

I live in a beautiful house in a nice neighborhood. I attend one of the best high schools in the country and have everything a girl could want except for one thing—my father is an active alcoholic.

Alcoholic—it used to mean skid row bums and dirty, rundown bars. Little did I know that alcoholics could be fine men like my father and that alcoholics "hung out" behind some of the nicest doors in town. Alateen straightened me out!

Alateen was working on me before I ever set foot inside a meeting. My group's sponsors live across the street from me. They started an Alateen group hoping my sisters and I would attend someday. It was through talks with these people that I began to understand my Dad's disease. Still, it took two years before my mother would let us go to meetings. She doesn't go to Al-Anon and was afraid how my father would react.

The night I came home from my first Alateen meeting, my heart was in my mouth. Everything turned out OK, but nothing has matched the fear I felt that first night on the way home.

For the first few weeks, my father seemed harder to live with. I think he felt we had turned against him.

Before I went to Alateen, I never realized how deeply I resented my father's drinking. As I look back now, I can remember my frequent tantrums, the tension that encompassed the whole house, the fear that plagued me daily. I didn't know why until I came to Alateen.

The greatest thing about Alateen is being with other kids who have the same problem and can truly understand how I feel. I have always felt that Alateen is the only place in the world where I can say "you know" and they know. Alateen is a place where taking and giving are one. I appreciate my family now more and more each day because the Alateen program has shown me where I was wrong.

Things Had To Get Worse

I wanted to be away from home as much as possible because I didn't enjoy being with anyone in my family. I thought this was normal.

When I was seventeen I found out that my father was an alcoholic But I was all right—or so I thought.

I began to hate my father because he was an alcoholic. In fact, I began to hate a lot of people. I found myself saying "I hate" more and more. Still, I thought I was normal. I started attending Alateen, but my brothers and sisters and I didn't think it was so bad in our house.

Things had to get worse before I could look at myself instead of others. When I did, I noticed I had as many faults as they did. Someone cared enough to listen to me and as I talked and lied to her I saw she had something really great—happiness and peace of mind. She told me to turn my life over to God. I couldn't even think of doing that. I thought I would turn into something really freaky.

Finally, one day when I was really low, I asked God to help me. He did. I still had the problem, but I felt better.

That was enough for a while, but soon that started to wear off. I had to keep working on myself. With God's help, I slowly changed and am much saner today. I don't hate anymore and I have learned to accept the family situation and myself. That was a lot to learn.

I Desperately Wanted To Be Loved

I have lived with a chronic drinking problem all my life. My father was not only an alcoholic but a drug addict as well.

The whole family was affected by his addiction to drugs and alcohol. I didn't realize it then, but I gradually became suspicious, sneaky and emotional. Even today, I hardly ever believe anything people tell me at first. I get upset because I think they are lying to me. But I am starting to develop self-confidence so this problem isn't as bad as it used to be.

I have always been jealous of my brothers because I thought they received more attention than I did. Even though a lot of the attention they got was rotten, I still envied them. I turned into a tomboy so I could do things with my Dad like my brothers did. It worked at first, but later they almost never wanted me to go along no matter how hard I tried. I felt deeply hurt.

Since neither of my parents spent much time with me, I became obsessed with a desire to be liked. I did everything to make others like me. When my friends put me down, I locked myself in a shell and sometimes didn't come out for weeks. I tried so hard to be liked that I never really had many friends.

When I was eight years old, the youngest of my three brothers was run over by a garbage truck in our driveway and was killed. Soon afterward, my mother came down with cancer.

We moved to another state to be near the best hospitals but we really couldn't do much for my mother no matter where we went. During this time, my mother gave me a lot of attention and I realized how much I loved her. My father was really great through her illness. A few months after we moved, she died.

We all went to live with relatives then and my father started falling apart. He didn't work and drank heavily. Since I didn't realize how sick he was, I lost respect for him. Somehow, though, I still loved him.

One day, my father was told to get a job or leave. The next day, we were on our way.

We then went to live with my father's parents but I hated it there. After two weeks, my father allowed me to go back and live with the relatives we had just left and told me to take one of my brothers along.

I knew how to get my own way there and boy did I! I went completely wild, coming home just to eat and sleep. My brother got most of the affection and I felt unlovable. I so desperately wanted to be loved and accepted that I tried to buy people's love. I even stole gifts for my family.

I seldom heard from my father and brother. One time, about two months went by without a word. I worried a lot about them. One night, I made a long distance call to my grandparents and found out that they had left a month earlier for California. I couldn't believe it—they were 3000 miles away. I resented not being told and got even wilder. Eventually, my father sent my other brother to live with us because he couldn't take care of him.

One day, my father called to say he was at the YMCA. For some reason, I thought of the YMCA as if it were the Salvation Army. I sensed that something was desperately wrong.

I received a letter from my father saying he was sorry for letting us down and that we'd have a new life together as a family. The next time I heard about him was when my grandparents called to tell us he had died.

The papers said he died after a long illness. That's true—his illness was addiction to drugs and alcohol. He killed himself. Before Alateen, I felt partly to blame.

After my father's death, we moved in with other relatives. The family situation wasn't the best and I started hanging out with wild kids. I started smoking dope to get them to accept me and ended up escaping all my problems that way. Even though I did everything I could to be accepted—stole, drank, did dope, gave money away—I still ended up a loner. Surprisingly, my school grades were good. But my attitude was lousy. I didn't care about anything and wanted to kill myself because I hated myself, my life and my family.

A few months ago I was turned on to the most beautiful way of life in the world—for me the *only* way—Alateen. Through Alateen and a drug meeting I attend, I got off drugs and began coping with my family problems in the right way.

No sooner had I really started to find myself in Alateen, than my relatives moved. I stayed with friends for two weeks while they got settled. For once in my life I really felt like someone. The most beautiful thing I found in those two weeks was God. This is the supreme thing you can get out of Alateen, and I'm thankful I've found Him. After two weeks alone, I moved down to my relatives' new home, leaving my Alateen group behind. But I took God and the program with me.

But all the problems came back. Everything went wrong. My faith in God started being torn down, the new life I had started to build began to crumble. I knew I must change the things I could.

So I did—God led me back home to Alateen. Since I'm 18, I left home and moved in with friends. Now I have my own apartment and a good job. I still attend Alateen every week.

About two months after I returned, I hit bottom. All of a sudden, I realized I wasn't really following the program; that I am sick. I had never admitted that before, but I'm glad I do now because I can start practicing the program without being phony. I thank God for letting me slip— He let me see how badly I needed Alateen.

I Couldn't Stand My Mother

My mother is not an alcoholic but she is a sick person. My father is an active alcoholic and his disease has spread through the whole family. I think my mother was most affected by his drinking, and she, in turn, affected me. She constantly worried and was nervous. I resented this because my friends' mothers were never like that. I resented her. I just did.

I even resented her sending me to my first Alateen meeting, but soon after that I began to understand that we were both sick.

I began to realize why I resented her and why I was scared of my father.

I am much more civil toward her now. I look to her for help in a lot of things. We are still not the best of friends, but at least I can accept and love her now just the way she is. Alateen has helped me to see where I was wrong and now I am working to make it right.

I Resented My Father's Death

My Dad was an alcoholic. Alcohol killed him. I started going to Alateen two weeks before he died. I was just beginning to understand that alcoholism is a disease and that I am not the only one with problems. I was beginning to accept the fact that my Dad didn't mean all the hateful things he did and said. My whole outlook on people, situations and life was changing. But I was confused. I wondered why these things had happened to me.

When my Dad died, I resented it. I couldn't understand why my father had to die; why he had to die so young. I suppose I was being selfish. I didn't look at it from my Dad's side. He was sick and in a lot of pain. He knew he was an alcoholic and was never at peace with himself. I know he hated himself for all the things that had happened. He tried to make up for all the bad but it was just too late.

Now that my father is dead, he doesn't have to suffer any more. He is at peace with himself.

His death caused a major crisis in our family. But everyone in Al-Anon and Alateen was really great and we realized there are people who do care.

Alateen has done so much for me besides helping me understand alcoholism as a disease, and accepting my father's death. I have learned to accept things for what they are. This is so important. I've learned how much one person can help another just by having lived through the same experiences. This is one of the reasons I continue to go to Alateen meetings. I'm not directly associated with alcoholism right now, but maybe I can help someone who is. And I can learn so many things from others. As long as I continue to learn, I'll keep going to Alateen meetings.

I Planned To Run Away

When I first came to Alateen I was just about ready to run away from home. My mother was drunk every night and a lot of the time during the day, too. I am sixteen years old but still I didn't know how I could get along by myself. My father had divorced my mother recently and I was put in her custody.

In Alateen I learned that my mother was sick and couldn't help getting drunk as soon as she took one drink. I learned, too, that I couldn't change her and would only make things worse if I tried. So I began to practice the 12 Steps and the Serenity Prayer. After a while my mother stopped drinking.

It would be fine if the story could end here, but it doesn't. My mother had stopped drinking before, and I knew she might not stay sober this time. Well, she didn't. She started drinking again after six weeks.

But what I want to say is that I am not as upset now by her drinking. I know I had nothing to do with it. I know she loves me in her own way. Someday I'll be through school and can get a job. By then I'll be independent and can make up my mind how and where I want to live.

I still get depressed and sometimes fall back into my old habits but now that I have friends who understand, to talk to, it's easier to begin again to practice the 12 Steps and the Serenity Prayer.

I still have quite a bit to change in myself. But thanks to Alateen, I have made a start.

Something Had To Give

My mother is the alcoholic in our family, but we are lucky because my father has stayed with us and tried to be both father and mother. Just the same, the whole thing was getting me down. I couldn't do my homework because my mother, who is in bed a good deal, kept calling me to get her a drink of water, or to help her to walk to the bathroom. I was afraid not to, for fear she would fall down and hurt herself.

But I was getting frantic. Something had to give and it looked like it was going to be me.

When I heard about Alateen, I went to a meeting and there other teenagers with my same problem talked to me. For the first time I realized that other people had the same difficulties I had. Other people were in school and trying to get decent marks, too. They explained that my mother was sick and that part of her illness was getting people to wait on her. This made her feel she was still important in the family and all of us cared about her and didn't want her to get hurt.

In Alateen I was told that I should let my mother get out of bed alone, even if she did fall down. They made me see that even if she hurt herself, she might need just that to make her realize she needed help. As long as she was protected she would make no effort to help herself, or to get help for her illness. In Alateen, I learned that I was *not* being kind by keeping my mother from facing her problem.

It was a different point of view to accept, but I feel it is the right one.

Like Mother Like Daughter

My mother was from a broken home where alcoholism was a major problem. I, too, have horrible memories of my father. He would beat my mother, threaten to shoot her with a .22 rifle. Sometimes he would go after me when he was drunk.

Finally my mother decided that divorce was her only choice. When she told my father this, he promised to join AA if my mother would stay.

Dad has been sober for ten years now. Through AA our home life became more peaceful and stable. I matured faster than most of my friends because of the problem I had had to face, but I was still very unstable. To outsiders I seemed well adjusted, but I knew something was missing. I didn't know how to help myself. Then I heard about Alateen.

I thought I was going only to help other teens who lived with an active alcoholic problem. Finally after about six months, all of my Alateen began to pay off. I found myself telling things I did not consciously realize had bothered me. I was so emotionally relieved that I cried. Here I was, Miss Know-it-all, admitting, to her own surprise, that she could give answers to others but was not able to keep herself from going to pieces.

Today I am wiser. I know I can not harbor resentments and fears. I think this has meant more to my maturing than any other single factor. I owe all this to the Alateen program.

I Have Two Alcoholics

There are two alcoholics in my home: my mother and my aunt, my mother's sister. My aunt's husband also lives with us, or perhaps I should say we live with him.

For a long time I hated everybody in the house; I hated everybody in school; and if I had ever gone any place else I'd have hated everyone there, too.

Once a boy I got to know in school did invite me on a hike in the country. His father drove us in their new car and we stayed overnight at *his* aunt's. But it was a lot different from *my* aunt's. They even had a swimming pool. They were fine to me but all the time I kept feeling sore that I had nobody of my own to take me out like that. I didn't know how to swim and I was mad because *my* home wasn't like theirs.

When I got back home our place looked worse than ever. My mother and my aunt were both drunk and I yelled at them. Then my aunt came at me and hit me and I hit her back. My uncle stepped in then and bawled me out and I was so mad I went to my room and locked myself in.

I'd gone to a few Alateen meetings but never had talked out, but a couple of nights after that fight I told the group about it. I thought they would feel sorry for me, but instead they told me my uncle was right, that I should never have gotten into a fight with an older person. If there was no other way to avoid a scene I should have gone out and walked around the block.

I did a lot of thinking after that and I listened harder to what the other teens had to say. And I began to open up to them. They sure did help me get a line on myself.

Now I don't fight with my mother or my aunt. I know

they are both sick. My uncle is sick, too, like I was. I wish he would go to Al-Anon. But I don't hate any of them any more. I have even joined a swimming class at the "Y". I've learned to enjoy what I can instead of being jealous of others.

When My Parents Got Sober, I Started Drinking

I first noticed our way of living was different from other people's when I was old enough to visit friends' homes. Their parents didn't have a glass of booze glued to their hands; everybody didn't yell at everybody else all the time! I was embarrassed by the way my parents were stumbling around and behaving, so I never had kids to my home.

Then my mother got fed up with the way she was living and started going to AA and Al-Anon. She found out that an Alateen group met near us every week, so I went to that—against my will at first, but when I learned to cope with my home situation, I couldn't wait until the next meeting! I learned my parents were sick and that they had a disease I couldn't control. I couldn't do anything about their lives, but I could do something about my own.

My father started going to AA a little while later, and it brought our family close for the first time.

But when I was fourteen, I got in with the wrong crowd and started drinking. I didn't drink to have a good time— I drank to be "in with the crowd" and most of all, I drank to get drunk. I even brought beer and a gang of kids into the house while my parents were at a meeting fighting to stay sober.

With the help of Alateen, I learned to find new friends who were really the right crowd. I thought I was "square" for a while, but I learned to like myself better—while I was drinking I really hated myself and the things I was doing.

Thanks to Alateen, I can talk to and understand people better, and I live what I call a happy, normal life. My parents and I have a good and open relationship, and they always listen if I have something to talk about. AA, Al-Anon and Alateen have brought us closer together.

We're All Like Sculptors

Sure, it was hard on us when the alcoholic drank—fights, no money and all that, but when he sobered up, the real work began.

Our family tried to pick up the pieces. We all tried to work together, but it was hard. We were all like sculptors trying to create a family, each with our own idea of what a family should look like. Each of us tried in his own way to help rebuild the family, but the many different ideas of what a family should be caused a lot of conflict.

That's where the AA, Al-Anon and Alateen programs were helpful. They helped us "get it all together" and head us all along the same track of recovery.

Sometimes, my arch enemy, self-pity sets in. It blinds me and makes me lose track of the program. If I give in to it, I become unsympathetic. I have no time to listen to the other guy's problems. I get selfish. As long as I am so absorbed with my own petty woes, I have no hope of getting better.

I try to overcome attacks of self-pity by concerning myself with others—not just within the program, but everywhere—at school, at home, in the neighborhood. Compassion, the program and help from my Higher Power pulls me through.

I Had To Learn To Love Myself

One thing my mother often said to me was, "Bonnie, why don't you like yourself? Your father and I love you." I knew they loved me, but I didn't know what she meant about liking myself. It just sounded conceited. Oh, I had days when I was glad to be alive, but I rarely knew what it was like to feel good about myself. Anyway, that was the general condition I was in at my first Alateen meeting. Feeling inferior and very unhappy, I listened but contributed very little. In those days my father was struggling for sobriety in AA and my mother was growing through Al-Anon. I then thought of alcoholism as a dirty, shameful word. I felt it was my father's problem, not mine. But I was wrong.

I left Alateen with a few resentments, but a lot of knowledge about alcoholism. Even so, I soon started on my own destructive route. My first drink was taken alcoholically, to escape pressures I had created. It wasn't long before I was smoking pot as well. I finished high school, but dropped out of night school and lost my job because of drinking. I tried AA then, but wasn't ready. When I left, it got worse, just as they had told me it would.

I went on to hard drugs. Then I got a higher paying job. I thought, "This is the life!" I couldn't have been more wrong. My family had been getting healthier around me, and I couldn't take their changes in attitude. I was disgusted with myself and my parents, so I left home and took an apartment with a girl friend. I didn't see much of my family after that. We were on speed, and after three months my friend and I were kicked out of the apartment.

Then my attitudes began to change. I found a one-room flat just for myself, and made plans for a new life of sobriety. But I was trying to do it all alone. In fact, I felt like the loneliest person on earth. Trying to be cheerful one day, I called my mother to invite her over to see my new place. I am sure today that it was a plea for help because when she asked me to come home, I nearly ran.

But once I was back home, I started my old pattern of drinking. Dad and Mom told me to either get help or leave. Thin, pale and distraught, I went back to AA. That was six months ago. I can only share my past with others. That is what I am doing in Alateen now. I know I cannot save some teens from going the same route I did, but I can help by letting them know that it can happen. I can share my strength, hope and experience, and pray that they too may find what I have found.

For the first time in my life, I'm starting to really care about other people, mainly because I feel like a worthwhile person. I believe the saying that you can't love someone until you first care about yourself.

I love my new life, and have so much gratitude. Alateen has helped me to see my own problem, and to save my life.

The Kids Used To Call Me "Stuck Up"

I was ashamed of my parents, my home and my life. To hide my feelings, I walked with my head high and my eyes to the ground. So I was called "Stuck-up"—all the time crying inside.

I wanted to ask the other kids to come over but I was afraid of what they might see if my father or mother were drinking. Dad was good and kind, very generous with whatever money he might have when he was drinking. But he was kind of messy, and I didn't want anybody to see that. When Mom drank, she was mean and ugly; and I didn't want that scene either.

I ran away from home when I was 12 to escape the belt beating Mom started to give me when I laughed at her. Today I know that it was the wine that made her act that way. She didn't really hate me. But at that time, I thought no one cared about me and I felt as though I hated my mother the most. I now know that's not true. I didn't hate her; I hated the things she did, especially when she was drinking.

In spite of all this, I managed to get excellent grades in school. But just before high school graduation, I gave up all hope of going to college, went into a depression, and quit school.

For a long, long time I blamed this on my parents. "If they didn't drink so much," I thought, "they would have seen to it that I had the proper clothes, that I went to basketball and football games, the school Proms and Balls, and did the things the other kids did." They didn't even seem to worry where the next meal was coming from—but I did!

So I went to work and earned my own money. But I put it all toward household expenses so that my younger brother and sisters would have something. All this did was feed my self-pity and fill my insides with bigger resentments.

The only boys my parents seemed to like were those who brought a bottle with them. In stories I had read, the fellow who dated a girl brought candy or flowers; not my dates! If they wanted to take me out, they brought booze for my parents. Boy, did I resent that!

Dad died a few years ago, but not before he had turned to ugliness and fighting when he drank. The once quiet, gentle man I remembered had become a brutal human being. He never accepted the help he was offered from AA.

Mom is still drinking, but I can see that each day she is getting sicker. I know the only thing I can do for her is pray. I no longer treat her as a blubbering idiot. She is my mother and I love her. Best of all, she seems to know it. Last Christmas, for the first time in my memory, she walked over to me and kissed me on the cheek without any warning.

I think my change in attitude has made the difference. It is my way of making amends. If I were to go to her and tell her how sorry I am for the past, she wouldn't understand.

With the help of Alateen, I am now trying to live one day at a time as best I can, grateful that I was able to change my life.

I Was A Plastic Person

Both my parents are alcoholics. Even though I can't remember them drunk, I do remember the worrying, crying and praying I did when they were drinking.

When my father drank, my mother would often leave home, taking me with her. I think the constant fear of where I would be living tomorrow messed me up the most. Whenever we left home, I would have to make friends all over again. But I was so unsure of myself, so afraid of not being liked, that I thought the only way to have people like me was to agree with them all the time, even if I didn't really feel that way. But it didn't work, and I felt awful. And so lonely.

So to get attention, I became outrageous. I did anything for a laugh. First, I pretended to be a great lover. I told everybody how great I was with the girls. But it wasn't true and I got uncomfortable with that story, so I decided to be a gambler. I lost, I stole, I quit.

Then I turned to drugs. I tried everything and became quite a mess. Thank God I never was addicted. But I did some really stupid things just the same. I sat naked on billboards, slept on bridges, and wore really weird clothes.

I went to Alateen, but I didn't tell the truth. As a result, I saw the others growing while I was still telling stories to get attention. Twice, I tried suicide. After a long time, I finally got honest. I told the group I had been a phony, a plastic person. I gave them the word about where I really was at. It helped me and really surprised me to find out how many people could identify with me.

Now I work the program the best I can. It's not all one big happy life. I still have doubts, fears and character defects. Taking my personal inventory scares me. I can see the things that are wrong with me. And because our group is really together, people will tell me if they see me go off the track.

I have changed quite a bit. It's easier for me to say "hello" to someone I don't know than it used to be. I have real, true and loving friends. I, too, am now capable of sharing my love with others, and feel sorry for those who have problems. I can now make decisions about my life and future. All I can say is, "Thank you."

I Was A Rebel

My mother was in the front room vacuuming. I wasn't sure if it was my birthday or not, so I asked her and got screamed at for asking the question. That was the extent of the birthday celebration and that was the way my whole life was.

I was constantly getting into trouble. I would try so hard to do things that would make my parents proud of me and happy but it just didn't seem to do any good. They are both alcoholics. It seemed to me that they didn't care about me. I decided that as long as I was going to get into trouble no matter what I did, I might as well do as I pleased.

The first time I got suspended from school was when I was in second grade. This was just the start of one continuous rebellion against authority. I rebelled against my parents, teachers, school officials, patrol boys, police and anybody in authority. I believed I was the boss.

I also developed a great need for attention. In order to get people to notice me, I made up wild stories. We were poor and I had to wear patched clothes to school. I guess I was the only one poor enough to dress like that, and it embarrassed me. School friends asked me about it, but I didn't want them to know that my parents didn't love me. I didn't want them to know that we were poor. So I told them I was an orphan and lived in a shack in the woods. I thought the way to make friends was to impress them. So I made up more and more wild stories. But the wilder the stories got, the fewer friends I had. Finally, I had none. I was so lonely. Everybody in my family was like that. The only friends my parents had were people like themselves. I thought nobody wanted me—not my parents, not my friends, nobody.

The only way I could live with myself from day to day was to say everybody else was wrong and I was right. I thought, "Nobody likes me, but I'm a nice guy. I guess *they* are all messed up." I didn't realize I was the one who was all messed up.

I finally was able to do one thing that impressed people—I became a very good diver. I could do a lot of really neat things. I was so pleased with myself and happy to finally get some recognition. Kids came up and asked me to show them how to do this or that; girls came up and said, "Isn't he cute?" I was good and I knew it. I got conceited about it. But the other kids wouldn't put up with this conceit. They say there is a sucker born every minute, and I took care of about two hours' worth. I fell for some of the dumbest things, and when everybody laughed, I just couldn't take it. So I was always in a fight. Even though I was smart, my grades were bad. I didn't give a damn. When I did try and got an outstanding grade, my father just said, "Why didn't you get a better grade?" So I decided, "To heck with it, I'll just do as I please," and I did.

We moved a lot and each time, I would think, "This time I'll get some friends." It never worked. I was always trying to impress people and all I did was turn them off. I guess they knew I was a phony.

This is the way my whole life went. If I wasn't in a fight with someone, I was in trouble with the law, my parents or the school. I couldn't figure out what was wrong with me. I remember one day kneeling down next to the bed and I cried. I wanted to know why we had to live the way we lived. No one could answer me because no one was there. I can't say I enjoyed a minute of my childhood. kept telling myself, "Tomorrow I'll be grown up and I'l be different and everyone will like me." But tomorrow never came.

I was constantly embarrassed by both my parents because they were always fighting in front of my relatives. Eventually, they were divorced. I was in 9th grade then. I went to live with my mother because I knew I would be able to smoke and do whatever I wanted. But it was the worst thing I could have done. I went to school when I felt like it. If the school officials called, I answered and said I was sick. The only people my mother associated with were other alcoholics. One night, we had a fight. I picked up the telephone and hit her in the eye with it.

She filed a complaint of assault and I was arrested. Jail was awful. I couldn't stand being caged up and thought I would go crazy. But it was good for me. I have never been in jail since and never want to be, either.

After that, I went to live with my father. But I couldn't adjust to high school. The only friends I had were hoods— guys who drank all the time, stole cars, the whole smear. I skipped school a lot more, had beer parties. My father often had to come and pick me up at the police station.

A girl who lived around the corner from me told me about Alateen. Her father was an alcoholic too. I went to humor her at first, but then I really liked it. This is where I belonged. These were my friends. This was where I could get straightened out. I was just one of the boys for the first time. I didn't want to be spectacular any more. I stopped looking for things in other people to pick at. I was looking for things in myself.

My father is now in AA. We get along like a father and son should. I have never seen him happier. Neither have I ever been happier. I am so grateful for what Alateen has done for me. I am no longer the kid everyone points to and says his old man is a drunk and he's really no better.

I Hid Behind My Father

When I was younger, I thought it was a normal, regular thing to drink. But later on, I knew that my father drank too much. I didn't want to make friends at school. I was afraid they might come to my house and find out what I knew. I just hid at home.

School didn't interest me. I didn't care. I never went anywhere. Why should I? I had no one to go with. No reason to want to go. I hated the school and the school hated me.

But I did have one friend. She had an alcoholic problem in her home too, so she knew how I felt. One day, we had a long talk. I realized I was just using my father's drinking as a big excuse because I was afraid to try to change. He was hiding behind the bottle and I was hiding behind him. I wanted to meet guys, go to dances and have a blast. Soon I would be on my own and I wouldn't be able to hide behind my Dad anymore. I had to face the world and everyone in it. I had to forget about my Dad. I had to face myself as I was—a scared little brat. I had to improve myself—things like what I said, how I said it, how I looked, everything. I had to care.

So I joined Alateen. Now I'm happy. I say "Hi" to everyone I know. I care how I look, and I have a social life. My father is not drinking but he is not in AA. My Mom's the greatest and goes to Al-Anon. We're a real family unit. We understand each other better.

My Mother And I Were Runaways

My parents are both alcoholics. When I was about

seven, my father's drinking got bad, so my mother and I left him. We stayed at my mother's friend's house for about three weeks and then went back home. That was only the first time. Four years later, we left again. This time we went to my grandmother's house and stayed for the summer. Then we moved into my aunt's three-room apartment. We didn't have much money, but my Mom sure tried. She used to get up at 6 o'clock to go to work. Our family was back together again before Christmas. But by the following September, my father was drinking again, so we left once more.

I hated it this time. I hated always having to make new friends. I was getting older and I needed my father more now. I missed him a lot. And I started to dislike my mother because of her drinking. It seemed that she was neglecting me more and more. Although I had everything I wanted, I didn't feel loved.

My father started taking me home for the weekend and I enjoyed those visits a lot even though he was still drinking. My friend and I used to play "Who can find the most wine bottles in the cellar."

In the meantime, my mother's disease was progressing. She was going to the bar three or four times a week. This lasted for about six months. Then one day she dropped me off at my father's house and he invited her in. Every time I visited my father, he would go out. I thought he was going to a bar, but for the last month, he had been coming home sober. Well, my mother walked in and was greeted by a man named Freddy. Freddy was a member of AA. I went out. When I came back, my father kissed my mother and I knew everything was all right. About a week later, we were all living together again. My mother went to Al-Anon and I went to Alateen.

The kids made me feel right at home. They didn't solve my problems, but told me how to overcome them. Alateens say what they think. If they think I'm wrong, they tell me. I learned I am powerless over alcohol, and began to detach myself from my parents' problems.

I use something Alateen has taught me every day. It helps me in school, at home, even on a football field. If I'm loaded down with homework, I don't get uptight. I say, "Easy Does It" or "First Things First." If I have a test, I say "Let Go and Let God." But I make sure I study for it!

Alateen has helped me overcome my faults: self-importance, self-pity, procrastination, self-justification and laziness. It has also helped me to admit when I am wrong.

In Alateen, I have met people who will probably be my friends for the rest of my life. I think Alateen is the best thing since apple pie. It sure is the best thing that ever happened to me!

HOW TO FIND OR START A GROUP

◆

If someone near and important to you is an alcoholic, and if you are a teenager, you can find help by joining an Alateen group. This can be done in one of several ways.

First, you may find a nearby group and attend its meetings. Don't hesitate because you're a stranger; anyone with this problem is welcome. You can locate a group by looking up an Al-Anon listing in the telephone book. If there is an Information Service or Intergroup, just call and someone will tell you which group is nearest you and when it meets. Or call any number listed under the name Al-Anon for this information. If none is listed, call AA. Usually the local Council on Alcoholism can also provide information about location and time of meetings.

If there is no Al-Anon group in your community, write to Al-Anon Family Group Headquarters, P.O. Box 182, Madison Square Station, New York, N.Y. 10159, for information and literature. Lone members in isolated areas all over the world learn about Alateen and how to practice its principles through corresponding with other members. The World Service Office can put you in touch with such friends-by-mail.

If there is an Al-Anon group near you but no Alateen group, you can urge the members to sponsor one. Information for Sponsors can also be obtained from the World Service Office.

LONERS' SERVICE

◆

There are teenagers who would like to join Alateen but cannot attend Alateen meetings—some because of poor health and many because there are no Alateen meetings in their neighborhood. They are directed to the Loners' Service.

These lone members are sponsored by Alateen members who are able to attend Alateen meetings on a regular basis. Through correspondence, they share with each other their hurts, strengths, program and hopes for the future. This correspondence broadens the view of the loner, who is unable to experience the comfort of sharing at meetings. Also, this special kind of Twelve-Stepping broadens the Sponsor's view, showing it is possible for the lone member to work the program even when there is no group available.

The *"Loners' Letter Box,"* a bi-monthly publication compiled of sharings from loners and Sponsors, is an active link in our efforts to help the lone member feel a part of the Alateen fellowship.

If you are interested in our Loners' Service as a loner or loner's Sponsor, please write to: Al-Anon Family Groups Headquarters, Inc., P.O. Box 182, Madison Square Station, New York, New York 10159.

ORGANIZING AN ALATEEN GROUP

◆

The organization of a group should be kept simple. Even a small group, however, needs a Chairman and a Secretary; sometimes the Secretary acts as Treasurer until the group is large enough to elect one. While the group is small, the Chairman may also act as Program Chairman. In a larger group, someone should be in charge of refreshments, setting up and cleaning up the meeting room. All officers are elected, usually for a term of three to six months or longer if the group wishes. Officers are trusted servants, not governors. Changing officers regularly gives all members the privilege of serving.

Duties of Group Officers

The Chairman
- plans meetings in advance with the Program Chairman
- opens the meeting by reading the Welcome or the Preamble, and leads the group in the opening and closing prayers
- introduces speakers or announces the subject of the meeting
- keeps the discussion on the right track

- makes sure everybody gets a chance to talk
- appoints committees when necessary

The Program Chairman

- books meetings and prepares the meetings in advance
- makes sure there is a good variety of topics so that there will be something for everybody and the meetings won't go stale

The Secretary

- handles group correspondence, such as sending announcements of anniversaries or other special meetings to neighboring groups and the Area newsletter if there is one
- notifies the World Service Office of any changes of mailing address
- picks up the mail from the post office box or permanent mailing address
- keeps an up-to-date list of members, their addresses and telephone numbers
- makes necessary announcements at meetings
- makes sure the group has enough literature and that it is well displayed at all the meetings
- uses the World Directory for group purposes and makes it available to other group members if they need it (for instance, if a member is going to another town and would like to attend a meeting there)

The Treasurer

- passes the basket at meetings
- takes care of the group's money and pays its bills

- asks another member to help count and record each collection
- keeps a record of all receipts and expenses
- makes a report to the group at regular intervals, usually once a month

The Group Representative

The GR, is the link to the World Service Office through the Area Assembly. He should be elected preferably for a three-year term. See *World Service Handbook for Al-Anon and Alateen Groups* for more detail.

The Information Service Representative

Where there is an Information Service (Intergroup), the groups may elect an ISR to represent them.

Sponsorship

Every Alateen group should have a Sponsor who is an active member of Al-Anon, and alternate Sponsors if possible. Former Alateen members are encouraged to start and sponsor Alateen groups while attending Al-Anon. AA members sometimes act as an assistant to the Al-Anon sponsor.

Groups do best when one sponsorship continues over a considerable period of time, at least a year and preferably two. The personal interest of Sponsors to whom the members can relate is of the highest importance. It is the Sponsor's responsibility to see to it that someone is there to replace him in the event he cannot attend the Alateen meeting.

It is not wise to have the parent of an Alateen member sponsor the group to which his child belongs. Members tend to talk less freely in the presence of a parent. The non-alcoholic parent, too, is often part of an Alateen's problem.

The Sponsor provides guidance in establishing the group's structure and functions: election of officers, planning the meetings, administration of funds, selecting and ordering literature, sending out notices, locating a meeting place, keeping in touch with absent members and the World Service Office. All this should be purely a matter of *guidance*, however. The members themselves should assume these responsibilities as soon as possible.

If a group should become dissatisfied with the Sponsor for a serious reason such as lack of interest or too much domineering interference with meetings, the members may decide to choose another Sponsor.

Suggestions for Sponsors:

- In the forming of an Alateen group the members may need some help, however, "Alateens are capable of conducting their own meeting and are well able to handle group responsibilities. They should be encouraged to do so.

- Sponsors may share their experiences with the Twelve Steps and knowledge of the Twelve Traditions; being careful not to take over the meeting by sharing too much. It's important for Sponsors to continue to go to Al-Anon meetings. This helps them to keep the focus of Alateen meetings on the Al-Anon program and aides Sponsors in answering questions asked by the teenagers.

- When asked questions about Al-Anon and Alateen policy, Sponsors can quote from Conference-Approved Literature, especially from the service manuals, instead of relying on their personal opinions.

- Since Alateen members often have other problems, Sponsors should be careful about giving advice; it is helpful, however, to know there are community resources available.

- Like Al-Anon, Alateen is anonymous and what is said at meetings is confidential. The Sponsor is not free to repeat what he or she hears whether at a meeting or on a one-to-one basis.

- Keeping in contact with other Alateen Sponsors can be supportive.

Meetings

To help with the transportation problem, Alateen groups may meet at the same place and time as an Al-Anon or AA group. Meetings should, of course, be held in separate rooms to assure privacy for each.

Groups which meet each week are apt to be more firmly established. Weekly meetings give members more opportunity to work on the program and apply it to their daily lives.

PLANNING A MEETING

♦

It's a good idea to plan different kinds of meetings. This way all the members can find something that appeals to them. If groups always have speakers, the members don't get enough chance to talk. If they always have discussion meetings, they never hear new ideas or points of view. Most groups find it's a good idea to discuss a Step and Tradition each month.

In some localities, exchange meetings are held to help the program chairmen of all the groups book speakers for their meetings. If no exchange meeting is held, the Program Chairman can use the World Directory to get in touch with neighboring groups in order to exchange speakers.

The following is a list of suggestions for meetings:

PERSONAL STORIES   The Chairman may ask two or three members beforehand to tell their stories, stressing how Alateen has helped them.

DISCUSSION MEETING   One or more of the 12 Steps and 12 Traditions, the Slogans, Serenity Prayer, or another appropriate topic can be discussed.

LITERATURE MEETING   An article from the *FORUM, ALATEEN TALK* or excerpts from Al-Anon or Alateen literature can be discusses.

PANEL DISCUSSION   A selected panel answers questions,

preferably written and unsigned to protect anonymity.

BUSINESS MEETING Business matters of the group can be discussed at the regular meeting if they are not too time consuming. Otherwise it is better if the officers of the group meet separately, either before or after the regular meeting.

EXCHANGE MEETING Your Alateen group can exchange speakers with another Alateen group. It's also helpful to have exchange meetings with Al-Anon.

OPEN MEETINGS may be held at various intervals, to which Al-Anon and AA members and any other interested persons are invited.

OUTSIDE SPEAKERS These may be members of Al-Anon or AA, doctors, ministers or social workers. They may be asked to speak if they are familiar with the program and the problems of alcoholism. It is a good idea to ask them to speak on a specific topic, and to make sure they understand our Traditions to prevent embarrassing situations. (See Tradition Eight). An occasional speaker from AA can be helpful.

SUGGESTED WELCOME

◆

We welcome you to the _____ Alateen Group and hope you will find in this fellowship the help and friendship we enjoy.

We who live, or have lived with the problem of alcoholism understand as perhaps few others can. We, too, were lonely and frustrated, but in Alateen we discover that no situation is really hopeless, and that it is possible for us to find happiness, whether the alcoholic is still drinking or not.

We urge you to try our program. We make no promises, but hope you will find solutions to your problems. So much depends on our own attitudes.

The family situation is bound to improve as we apply the Alateen ideas. Without spiritual help, living with an alcoholic is too much for most of us. We become irritable and unreasonable without knowing why.

The Alateen program is based on the Twelve Suggested Steps of Alcoholics Anonymous which we try, little by little, one day at a time, to apply to our lives along with our Slogans and the Serenity Prayer. The love and sharing among members and daily reading of Alateen and Al-Anon literature helps to bring us serenity.

Like AA and Al-Anon, Alateen is an anonymous fellowship. Everything that is said here, in the group meeting and member-to-member, must be held in confidence. Only in this way can we feel free to say what is in our minds and hearts, for this is how we help one another in Alateen.

SUGGESTED CLOSING

◆

In closing, I would like to say that the opinions expressed here were strictly those of the person who gave them. Take what you liked and leave the rest.

The things you heard were spoken in confidence and should be treated as confidential. Keep them within the walls of this room and the confines of your mind.

A few special words to those of you who haven't been with us long: Whatever your problems, there are those among us who have had them too. If you try to keep an open mind, you will find help. You will come to realize that there is no situation too difficult to be bettered and no unhappiness too great to be lessened.

We aren't perfect. The welcome we give you may not show the warmth we have in our hearts for you. After a while, you'll discover that though you may not like all of us, you'll love us in a very special way—the same way we already love you.

Talk to each other, reason things out with someone else, but let there be no gossip or criticism of one another. Instead, let the understanding, love and peace of the program grow in you one day at a time.

Will all who care to, join me in the closing prayer?

REMEMBER!

◆

1. We have been brought together by one common problem; let us concentrate on that. Religion, politics or other such topics have no place in our group.
2. Resist the temptation to gossip, and discourage it in others. Anything that is hurtful to one member detracts from the strength of the group, as well as the person responsible. It is this strength on which every member depends for help in meeting problems.
3. No one should take on a bossy attitude toward other members, directing the group's activities, giving advice, or making decisions without consulting the others. Although members may be given certain responsibilities, all are equal.
4. Be patient with those who are slow to grasp the principles of the Alateen program. Each person must progress in his or her own way and time. We all help each other by telling our experiences in order to throw light on others' problems.
5. Never forget that the Alateen meetings are working sessions with the serious purpose of helping us to make our lives happier and more serene. Let us not defeat its purpose by wasting time on fun and games. Socializing should be reserved for other occasions.
6. Keep in confidence everything that is said at meetings.

If members are assured that what they tell will not be revealed outside the group, they will feel encouraged to speak freely. Knowing that "you can tell anything" to fellow Alateens will have rich rewards for all. The friends you make in Alateen are special.

THE VOICE OF ALATEEN IS HEARD

◆

Alateen groups are actually Al-Anon groups for teenagers. Each Alateen group has the same rights and privileges as an Al-Anon group. To understand what that means, we are outlining here the basic structure of Al-Anon Family Groups. For more information, please read *Al-Anon and Alateen Groups at Work* and *The World Service Handbook for Al-Anon and Alateen Groups*.

As of 1981, there are over 15,000 Al-Anon and 2,258 Alateen groups in the world registered with the World Service Office in New York City. The *WSO* prints and distributes all of the official Al-Anon and Alateen literature. It helps new groups get started, publishers a World Directory, which is sent free to each group annually, prints and distributes The *FORUM*, a monthly magazine of stories and letters from members all over the world and prints and distributes *ALATEEN TALK*, a bimonthly newsletter for Alateens. Volunteer committees at the *WSO* guide the membership everywhere in matters of Policy, Public Information, Alateen and Institutions.

Our Traditions say that the "group conscience" is the ultimate authority in our fellowship. They say further that our service boards and committees are responsible to those they serve. That means that although we have a central office in New York City, the people who work in that office are not our bosses but our trusted servants. Their job is to service the groups, not run them. They guard the Traditions and promote the growth of Al-Anon and Alateen world-wide. They find out what the groups want and do their best to provide it.

How can they do this? It isn't possible to write to all the groups every time a decision has to be made! That was how they did it in the beginning. But the fellowship is much too big now for that method to be practical. So the annual World Service Conference was set up to bridge the communication gap.

In the spring of each year, the members of the World Service Office meet with the Delegates from all over the United States and Canada to discuss Al-Anon and Alateen worldwide. The Delegates find out what the World Service Office is doing and the World Service Office finds out what the groups are doing and what they want and need. Of course, the Delegates don't have to wait until the Conference to have a question answered. They are in touch with the World Service Office throughout the year.

How is a Delegate selected? It starts with the groups. Each Al-Anon and Alateen group elects a Group Representative (GR). The Group Representatives elect a District Representative (DR) and a Delegate. A Delegate represents an Area, usually a state or province. Some states and provinces have so many groups that they divide into two Areas, each one with its own Delegate. The District Representatives are the links between the Delegates and the Group Representatives. Instead of visiting each group in the Area, the Delegate can call a meeting of District and Group Representatives to tell them about the Conference and to find out about group problems.

Every group has a voice. Every group gets the same service. Every group has an equal share of responsibility.

ALATEEN COMES OF AGE

◆

In the Beginning

Alcoholics Anonymous was founded in 1935. As groups sprang up and began to hold meetings around the country, the spouses of these AA members also began to meet at the same time.

They discovered that they had many problems in common, and that they could apply the Twelve Steps and the Slogans of AA to themselves. Little by little, their meetings took shape as study groups, with the members working the AA program in order to improve their own personalities and attitudes.

In 1951, a handful of these scattered family groups around the United States finally came together in an organization which they agreed to name *Al-Anon Family Groups*. Their purpose was to help the families of alcoholics, through the use of the Twelve Steps and Twelve Traditions which they adopted from AA.

As early as 1954, the special problems of young people were a major concern. In that year, Al-Anons planned talks on this subject to be given at the 1955 AA Convention in St. Louis. The session was called "Children of Alcoholics."

ALATEEN STEPS INTO THE PICTURE

In 1957, the first Alateen group was formed in California by Bob, the teenaged son of AA/Al-Anon parents. The group flourished. Patterning its program on Al-Anon's, the members used the Steps, Traditions and Slogans as they applied to the needs of the teenaged children of alcoholics.

Alateen grew year by year. Soon Al-Anons around the world, aware of the importance of this movement, spread the word that there was help for the troubled young people who were living with the problem of alcoholism.

The year of Alateen's beginning, the World Service Office published the first Alateen booklet, *Youth and the Alcoholic Parent*. A year later, a chapter on Alateen was added to the basic Al-Anon book, LIVING WITH AN ALCOHOLIC.

Articles appeared in magazines and newspapers; more Alateen literature was printed, its content influenced by the Alateens themselves. By the end of 1960, the World Service Office was servicing 115 groups.

The progress continued at an increasing rate. Groups sprang up in Africa, Australia, Europe and South America. Each year more literature was distributed, more letters written, more interest indicated by professionals, and more Alateens were represented at AA/Al-Anon Conferences and Conventions. Eventually, Alateen Conventions were planned, financed and attended by Alateens and their sponsors.

Alateen groups were not without problems, however. Growth was hampered by the reluctance of Al-Anons to undertake the sponsoring of groups. Many groups disbanded for various reasons. But by and large, the solid growth and expansion continued, and many Alateen members who had become too old for Alateen joined Al-Anon and sponsored new Alateen groups. Alateen has now come of age. Alateen members and groups enjoy the same privileges and share the same responsibilities as Al-Anon groups do in the fellowship. They are full-fledged Al-Anon groups for the younger members of the family.

A statement by a Delegate to the World Service Conference puts in a nutshell the relationship of Alateen and Al-Anon:

"Alateens are the fortunate *early* members of the Al-Anon fellowship. Belonging to Alateen is the first step in developing spiritual awareness and maturity. The Alateen is passing through this stage. When he has outgrown his teen years, his interests will no longer be so closely involved with Alateen matters. He will continue to practice the program in Al-Anon with his age peers, and with them, help a new generation of teens embrace this radiant philosophy."

ALATEEN HIGHLIGHTS

1957 First groups started. Literature: *Children of Alcoholics, Youth and the Alcoholic Parent,* reprint of AA *Grapevine* article: *It's a Teenaged Affair, Alateen Traditions.* All new literature announced in The *FORUM,* Al-Anon's monthly publication, sent free to all Al-Anon and Alateen groups.

1958 Groups total 45. Alateen Committee was established at the World Service Office.

1959 Articles appeared in magazines and newspapers.

Chapter on Alateen was added to LIVING WITH AN ALCOHOLIC.

1960 Alateen workshop at the International AA Convention in Long Beach, Cal.; transcript was added to literature list. More magazine articles. New literature: *Operation Alateen* written by Alateens. Free copies to all groups.

1961 Groups total 154. Material provided by Al-Anon for articles in *Life* magazine, *Time, American Weekly, Children's Family Digest, Guideposts, Seventeen, The Messenger, Inventory,* and *Teen Etiquette;* all resulting inquiries answered and free literature sent.

1962 Survey conducted among Alateen groups by WSO, reported in the *FORUM* and included in the World Service Conference Delegates Brochure. Groups started at correctional institutions. Alateen meeting at New Jersey AA Convention. First all-Alateen Conference held. TV showings on two major networks arranged by Alateen Committee. Over 350 inquiries received as a result of magazine articles.

1963 Groups total 262. New groups in India, England, Puerto Rico, Australia, New Zealand. New literature: *A Guide for Alateen Sponsors, For Teenagers with an Alcoholic Parent.* Alateen Conference held in Boston. Publicity continued, literature constantly updated.

1964 Increased growth in U.S., Canada and internationally requires the addition of a full-time Alateen secretary to the World Service Office staff. Many inquiries received as the result of newspaper articles. Six WSC Delegate members added to Alateen Committee. Alateen Conference in Syracuse, N.Y. Several institutional groups added. Reprints of article in

Youth magazine, *Alcohol, Alibis and Alateen* added to literature list. *ALATEEN TALK,* newsletter named by a vote of the groups, first published by the WSO, sent free quarterly to all Alateen groups.

1965 Groups total 315. Alateen conferences at Haverford, Pa., with 20 groups represented, and Huntsville, Ala. Numerous groups represented at AA/Al-Anon Conventions in U.S. and Canada.

1966 New groups: 195, including Mexico, Honduras, Zambia (Africa), and Australia. Many letters from professionals. Continued and increased participation of Alateen in fellowship Conventions. National publicity included articles in *Seventeen, Redbook, McLeans, Pageant, Scope* and *Teen Magazine.*

1967 New groups: 124, including France and Finland. Articles in *Parents Magazine, Teen* and *AA Grapevine.* Programs on radio and CBSTV, the latter also subject of an article in the New York Times. Alateen secretary interviewed by CBS news. Much publicity in pamphlets, booklets and bulletins by community organizations. Alateen represented at conventions in California, Texas, Ontario and British Columbia. Workshop at bilingual convention in Quebec.

1968 New groups: 245; Overseas groups in Scotland, Australia, Finland, Mexico, South America. Alateens and sponsors spoke at a maximum security prison in Canada. Members in California addressed a teachers' meeting, opening the way for much message-spreading in high schools. Alateen represented at Conventions in California, Connecticut, Florida, New York, Texas, British Columbia, Ontario and Quebec. Many Assembly Areas appoint or elect Alateen Committees and/or Coordinators. Two pieces of literature authored by Alateens added to literature list: *Step Four Inventory* and *Suggested Programs for Alateen Meetings.* Free copies sent to all registered groups; also included in free starter packet. Ann Landers mentioned Alateen twice; result, over 700 letters. Earlier Landers article reprinted in *Readers Digest.* World Service Conference Delegates actively promoting Alateen in their Areas. *It's a Teenaged Affair* published in French. Alateen Conferences in Texas and Saskatchewan.

1969 Groups total 701. New groups in Colombia, South America; Edinburgh, Scotland; Victoria and Queensland, Australia; Finland, Mexico and Puerto Rico. First Texas Alateen Conference held in Brownwood and First Saskatchewan Alateen Conference held in Saskatoon. French Literature Committee reported 31 French-speaking groups and nine Lone Members. Growing interest in structure of fellowship and participation in District meetings. Alateens continue to carry the message to guidance counselors, social workers, public school assemblies, church groups, etc.

1970 New groups: 259, including Nicaragua, Finland, Germany, South Africa, England, Eire, Spain, Holland and Belgium. *ALATEEN TALK* printed bimonthly. Alateen booklets translated into Spanish and Finnish. Alateen's part in the AA International Convention in Miami: 3 Workshops and Alateen speakers at two Big Meetings. Over 400 inquiries answered and literature samples sent. Three new regional Conferences on the Eastern Seaboard. New literature: *Do's and Don'ts* and *A Guide for Alateen Speakers,* written by Alateens.

1971 Groups now number 850; 198 Lone Members and Contacts. More literature translated into French and Flemish. UK and Eire reported Alateen participation in European AA Convention. Four-part Alateen Workshop at the World Service Conference. Increased interest on the part of Alateen to participate at the District and Assembly level. Changes in *World Service Handbook* clarify Alateen role in over-all structure; copies sent to all groups. Requests for direct representation at the World Service Conference by members of Alateen Conferences were brought up for consideration at the World Service Conference. Alateen members joined both Literature and Alateen Committees. French Literature Committee now serving 35 groups in Quebec; other French-speaking groups in Switzerland, France and Belgium.

1972 Groups reach 1,000. Teen members developed *Alateen Just For Today* into a wallet-size card.

1973 ALATEEN—HOPE FOR CHILDREN OF ALCOHOLICS, Alateen's first hardcovered book; a pamphlet, *Alateen Twelve Steps and Twelve Traditions;* and "Guidelines for Alateen Coordinators" make their first appearance.

1974 The Alateen Committee approves a mimeographed sheet, "What's Expected of an Alateen Sponsor?" The cartoon feature "Mei 'n Mutt" is included in *ALATEEN TALK.*

1975 Recurring requests for registration and service of separate preteen groups result in Area-wide surveys. The World Service Conference votes to continue the policy which encourages younger family members to join an Alateen group which, by autonomy, may divide its meeting into age segments. Alateen Conferences total 18. A special committee draws up "Suggested Guidelines for Alateen Conferences." New Literature: a cartoon booklet, *If Your Parents Drink Too Much*. Greater Alateen participation at Denver AA International and a first: AA asks for an Alateen Speaker at one of *their* meetings.

1976 Almost 2,000 groups now registered. An Assistant Alateen Secretary is added to the staff. *ALATEEN TALK* is expanded to 6 pages and sent to all Al-Anon groups to encourage their active participation in Alateen.

1977 Alateen celebrates its 20th Anniversary! The history of Alateen is featured in *ALATEEN TALK* throughout the year. New literature includes a children's book, What's "Drunk," Mama?, to be used as a shared reading experience with younger children; and the Alateen Program Card, a wallet-sized reprint of the 12 Steps and Alateen's 12 Traditions. Also developed is a mimeographed "fold-it-yourself" sheet with suggested "Try To's and Try Not To's for Sponsors and Co-Sponsors of Alateen Groups."

1978 A skit is presented to the World Service Conference titled, "Saturday Night Sponsor Fever." The suggestions and solutions to questions asked after each act are to be part of a proposed pamphlet already in progress. Copies of the play are sent to groups for local presentations.

1979 "Al-Anon—A Continuation of Alateen Growth" is the Alateen Committee's presentation to the World Service Conference. Alateens are encouraged to go on to Al-Anon as they grow older and Al-Anons are encouraged to accept these former Alateens. A Loners'

Service was developed for teenagers in need of the Alateen program, but without a nearby meeting. Through correspondence, Alateens who attend meetings share their program and experience with Lone Members.

1980 A new statement on Alateen Membership was voted upon and accepted at the 1980 World Service Conference. It covers an expansion of Alateen, which would be known as "pre-Alateen". Alateen participates in the 1980 AA International Convention in New Orleans.

ALATEEN LITERATURE

◈

All literature published by Al-Anon Family Group Headquarters, Inc. (The World Service Office) has the approval of the World Service Conference and is so identified. It is suggested that only approved publications be used in studying the Alateen program and particularly at Alateen meetings. Alateen members are urged to make use of the Al-Anon literature, but this book and several leaflets and pamphlets have been written just for them. A catalog and price list are available on request.